THE
Woodworker's Kitchen

24 Projects You Can Make

A.J. HAMLER

POPULAR WOODWORKING BOOKS

CINCINNATI, OHIO

popularwoodworking.com

CONTENTS

◆

SERVING

ACCESSORIES

INTRODUCTION

◆

MOST WOODWORKERS WILL tell you that their shop is their favorite place in the world, and rightly so. But imagine a woodworker with two shops. Say what? Two shops? What woodworker has two shops?

Well, I do.

My first shop is a converted extralarge two-car garage attached to my house, and it has just about everything I need to build just about anything I want. But the best part is that because the shop is attached to the house, all I have to do is walk through a door and I'm in my second workshop: my kitchen.

I've been cooking almost as long as I've been woodworking – or is that the other way around? There's nothing I like better than wrapping up a great project my first workshop, and then capping off a perfect day by spending time in my second.

As woodworkers, we love making things for our homes. And, while all the woodworking magazines run projects for the kitchen from time to time, it occurred to me that a collection of these projects would appeal to those of us who enjoy creating things at both the table saw and the stove.

PROJECTS

Coming up with projects was easy – I think my initial list had about a hundred possibilities – but selecting two dozen proved a bit more difficult. So I looked at what we do and

use in the kitchen, and decided to break it down into four categories.

The first three fall in a logical order. Before cooking everything we need is put away, so the first section of the book covers kitchen items related to storage. After that are projects relating to the actual preparation and cooking process, followed by a section devoted to serving a meal.

Throughout this process, though, are a number of kitchen and cooking items that could fall into more than one section – the Kitchen Island and Paper Towel Holder would be at home in all of them – so I thought a category for general accessories was a good match for those in the fourth section.

The one thing that ties every project together is that they're all intended to complement and work with things you already have in your own kitchen. Others are designed around specific types of hardware or other non-wood materials you'll need to purchase.

As such, every one of the projects is intended to be customized for your space, how you work, and with availability of hardware and other items in mind. So even though I give exact measurements for everything, these dimensions are intended to be fluid.

Sometimes the included measurements are optimal for best usage, such as the Silverware Organizer being sized to fit a standard kitchen drawer. Other times, though, hard-

ware or other items determined the size. For example, the Spice Rack accommodates the particular bottles I got for it, while the slots in the Knife Block were positioned and sized to accept the knives I already own.

For that reason, begin every project with your tape measure or rule.

I've sized the projects to match my needs and space, as well as the objects being used with them, but yours may be different. Cabinet clearances, countertop shapes and areas, drawer

Before starting any project you plan to use with something you own or buy specifically for the project, always get accurate measurements and adjust project dimensions accordingly.

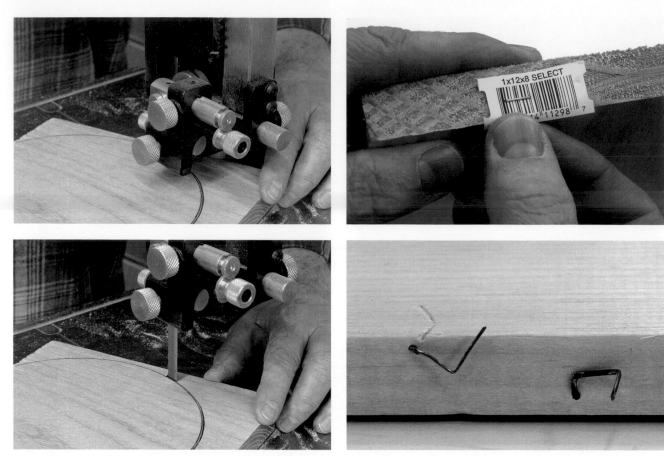

In proper use, a band saw's guide post rides close to the workpiece, but I've raised it to give a better look at the procedure being performed.

Be extremely careful with home center lumber, as you'll frequently find lots of staples on the wood's edges.

sizes and locations, sink and even utensil dimensions could all make a difference, so measure first then tweak project dimensions and details for a perfect fit.

SAFETY

Woodworking has inherent dangers, and although being safe has a lot to do with common sense and simply paying attention, there are a number of specific safety practices that should never be violated. I mention safety a number of times for specific processes throughout this book, but here are a few things to keep in mind right from the beginning.

Follow all general safety rules, such as providing adequate lighting in your work area at all times, as well as sufficient ventilation when working with glue, paint and finishes.

Above all, be sure to protect your eyes and ears.

You'll notice on many of the projects where I've used a band saw to cut workpieces, that I've raised the guide post pretty high. This is for photographic reasons only so you can see what's going on in the process being shown. However, for both safety and adequate control of the cut, always set your guide just above the surface of the wood when working with the band saw.

Likewise, you'll notice I've removed the guard on my table saw for photographic clarity. In your own shop, you should always use guards and other safety devices whenever working with power tools.

There are a lot of sharp edges involved in woodworking, but a new one has become a personal pet peeve of mine: staples. Stickers can fall off,

so home centers now staple price tags on the ends of lumber. Be sure to remove these before working with the lumber, as they can ruin blades if you inadvertently cut through them. If whoever put the staple there wasn't careful, one end of the staple may have missed the wood and be sticking out just waiting to skewer an unsuspecting finger.

Even more distressing is the practice of driving multiple staples along wood edges, "bridging" boards to keep them from sliding when shipped and stacked. When boards are separated staples pull free on one end, leaving sometimes dozens sticking out. Be aware of these when grabbing lumber out of the racks and remove before working the lumber. (Tip: Slip a pair of pliers into your pocket before you go shopping, and pull those nasty things out even before you buy the wood.)

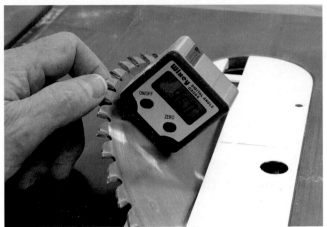

On the left is an end and face view of cherry, a typical closed-grain hardwood. At right is oak, an open-grained hardwood that shouldn't be used for food-contact projects.

A digital angle gauge is infinitely more reliable than a tool's built-in gauges.

Thes are typical woodworking screws you'll find at any home center or hardware store.

To hide screws, use a countersink bit or a combo bit that drills both a pilot hole and countersink at the same time.

WOOD

As with all woodworking projects you'll choose wood for two main reasons, appearance and appropriate strength/durability for the intended use. However, for kitchen projects you need to add another criteria, and that's whether there will be direct food contact.

For projects where food comes into contact with the wood, especially for preparation involving raw meat, closed-grain hardwoods are best. Open-grained woods like oak often have hollow pores that sometimes run the length of the wood. When cut, these open pores leave a grooved surface no matter how much you sand it smooth. Not only will food readily lodge in this open grain, but liquid can wick deep into

the wood. Closed-grained woods like maple and cherry, on the other hand, minimize the chance that food will remain embedded in the surface.

It's also best for most of these projects to stick with hardwoods. You'll find that hardwood lasts longer, provides a smoother surface finish and, because hardwoods are denser and generally less porous, they don't soak up food liquids as quickly as softwoods. It's the best choice for any kitchen project that makes actual contact with food or cooking processes.

Exotic lumber always lends a beautiful appearance, and the high density of many exotics allows polishing to a high sheen even without finishing. However, some exotics like those in the rosewood family are

extremely oily. These can present glue issues, not what you need for anything exposed to water. Also, this oiliness may affect the type of finish you choose. Some finishes simply don't dry well on exotics and remain sticky forever. A finish like mineral oil – which doesn't dry at all – can be a slimy mess on an oily exotic.

TOOLS & TECHNIQUES

We've assumed throughout the projects that you have a reasonable proficiency with woodworking techniques and skills, so this book isn't intended to be a woodworking tutorial. However, here are a few tips that will make spending time in the shop more efficient and pleasurable.

A lot of tools come with built-in

Salad bowl finish is an excellent wiping varnish, but has no magical "food safe" properties. All clear finishes are food safe once cured.

gauges, but I've found their accuracy to be notoriously unreliable. For that reason, I just don't trust them and use a digital angle gauge instead. These have a button to zero them out on the cutting surface, and then when transferred to the blade – or the other way around in the case of a tilting table – give a spot-on angle every time. I wouldn't make a beveled cut without one.

There aren't a lot of fasteners used in these projects, as most rely on the strength of a particular type of joinery (or simply don't have joints). If you do use screws, keep in mind that the kitchen or backyard grill can be a wet environment during preparation and cooking, especially during cleanup. For that reason, avoid common black screws, sometimes called "drywall screws," in favor of coated screws. Bright zinc-coated screws are fine for indoor furniture items, but for anything that has the potential for repeated direct contact with water exterior-grade screws are best.

When you do use screws, always countersink them. Not only does this help to keep them out of the way of water and food, it simply looks better.

If I need to cut identical parts,

such as the opposite sides of a box or multiple dividers that are all the same size, whenever possible I like to stack them together and cut them simultaneously. Some painter's tape wrapped around the edges holds the pieces firmly together as a unit, and you can cut right through the tape with no issues. A stop on a table saw or other tool can help to cut identical parts, but cutting or shaping two or more at the same time guarantees they'll be exactly the same. What's more, with the parts taped, you'll only need to measure and mark (or transfer cutting patterns) on just the top workpiece in the stack. You'll see this a lot throughout the book.

Presentation faces should be oriented upward and outward; secondary faces downward and inward. This is particularly important for cutting surfaces and kitchen furniture with visible tops.

Finally, water-resistant or waterproof glue is best for any project that is washed or otherwise gets wet or regularly handles moist or drippy items, like a cutting board. In fact, I've used it for all the projects that you'll see.

FINISHES

Strictly speaking, many kitchen items don't need a finish. Some take such a beating and are thoroughly washed so often that you may want to skip it all together. However, a good finish can help protect items that receive frequent washing and keep them looking good. More importantly, finishing wood helps prevent the natural moisture found in food from getting into the wood.

Moisture is a wonderful carrier for bacteria, so the last thing you want with a food-contact item is for bacteria to be left behind. Keep in mind, too, that while moisture tends to give an image of something in liquid form, it applies equally to things like tiny bits of raw meat and vegetables. We've addressed that earlier by stressing that only closed-grain wood should be used

for food-contact items, but you can add additional protection.

By applying a finish you help the wood slow the absorption of water. When washed after cooking, food items clean more easily if nothing has absorbed into the wood. Finished items also dry more quickly after washing, further helping to prevent bacteria from getting a foothold.

But what kind of finish do you use? Every finish that comes in a can carries seemingly dozens of warnings as to the scary contents. As a result, woodworkers seem on a constant quest for a finish that is food safe. More often that not, the recommendation is to use a natural finish such as walnut oil, mineral oil or paraffin wax.

These finishes are fine, if you like them, although mineral oil never really dries. Wooden items treated with mineral oil will always look dull and feel odd to the touch. It also washes off and needs regular replenishing. Wax rubs off in use fairly quickly, too. However, in the interests of kitchen items being food safe, many woodworkers will use nothing else.

The other commonly recommended solution is to use a coating sold as a salad bowl finish. Years of marketing has given the impression that salad bowl finishes are somehow different than others, with special food-safe qualities. The idea is so ingrained that many woodworkers swear it to be true.

However, salad bowl finishes are nothing more than wiping varnishes – simple varnish that has been thinned about 50 percent. The ingredients are pretty much the same as any other wiping varnish available today.

The key is that salad bowl finishes are marketed as being food-safe or non-toxic when cured. But here's the thing: All modern clear finishes are food-safe when cured. You pick the finish – alkyd or polyurethane varnish (wiping or not), Danish or tung oil finishes, boiled linseed oil, shellac, lacquer – all of them are non-toxic when fully cured.

Wiping varnishes and oil/varnish blends are fine choices for kitchen items.

You wouldn't want to drink any finish out of the can, as in liquid form you'd be chugging down solvents or metallic driers added to the finish. But the curing process eliminates any dangers with both; solvents evaporate and disappear, while metallic driers (which are minimal to begin with) become contained as part of the curing process.

The important thing to remember is that the finish must be fully cured. Package directions have a wide range of recommended cure times, but actual cure time can vary with temperature and humidity. There's also a difference between "dry" and "cured." An object may be dry enough to handle in just a few days (or even hours for some finishes), but curing takes longer. The best way to tell is simply to smell it – if you can still smell solvent, it's not cured yet.

For kitchen items that don't contact food, you can use whatever clear finish, or even paint, that you want. For food-contact items like cutting boards and utensils, if the goal is appearance, most oils work well to bring out the beauty of the wood and offer a modicum of water protection. These finishes soak into and cure in the wood, not in a film on the surface like a thick varnish or shellac will. With washing, these may need to be recoated periodically.

Oil/varnish blends like Danish oil offer a bit more protection, as well as a higher sheen if that's what you're looking for. While sturdier than plain oils, these may also need to be replenished after repeated washing. These can build a thin film with several applications, but it can be abraded and washed off over time

For the highest protection, an alkyd or polyurethane varnish is best. Keep in mind that varnishes are film-building finishes that leave a hard, clear coat on top of the wood that forms a barrier. This is great for wear and tear (and water protection) for kitchen items that are frequently handled, or for furniture items like the Kitchen Stool and K-Cup Center.

Varnishes aren't that good for use where the surface is regularly abraded, however, such as a cutting board.

Even with only a few weeks use, a varnished surface on a cutting board will be sliced through repeatedly. The whole point of finishing is quickly lost: Moisture will go right through the cuts in the finish and down into the wood.

For these, I like to use a wiping varnish or oil/varnish blend that I thin a bit further with mineral spirits. The thinned nature really allows it to soak rapidly into the wood where it cures beneath the surface. I generally flood on as much as it will take, replenishing any spots where it soaks all the way in. After 20 minutes or so I wipe every bit of excess off the surface and allow it to dry for a day or two.

After that I repeat the process until finish no longer soaks in. When it's cured completely, I go over it with very fine sandpaper or steel wool to remove any surface film. A cutting board finished like this won't be literally waterproof, but it'll be the next best thing.

KITCHEN STORAGE

✦

AN ORGANIZED, ATTRACTIVE KITCHEN IS THE FIRST STEP TO
spending an enjoyable time cooking. ✦ Sure, you can toss things into
any available drawer or cabinet, and you probably have plenty of those.
But trying to find just what you want when you need it in a cluttered
drawer or on a disorderly countertop takes a toll on the creative experience. Having a specific place or means of storing utensils, supplies and
other kitchen gear not only makes good sense, it makes the entire process easier – and a lot more fun. ✦ So before we start cutting veggies,
turn on the stove or even decide what culinary magic we want to create,
let's take a look at six ideas for keeping your kitchen in order.

✦

Modular Spice Rack

WHEN IT COMES TO KITCHEN accessories, probably the first thing that comes to mind is a spice rack. Almost every kitchen has one, if for no other reason than it's the quintessential wedding or housewarming gift. But what if you want a spice rack but you've neither gotten married nor moved into a new home lately? You go out and buy one.

No, wait – this book is all about making your own kitchen items, so of course that's exactly what we'll do. (I was joking about the "go out and buy one" thing.)

I chose a spice rack as the lead project not only because of its timeless nature as a classic kitchen storage accessory, but also because the process of making one uses several techniques you'll see throughout this book. As such, it seemed the perfect project to start with.

This is a small rack with two levels of five bottles each, but instead of a solid unit I've made it so the two levels are separate with one stacking atop the other. The sides, each cut from a single piece of stock, feature continuous grain top to bottom. When not in use, just stack and store the rack. However, I find it easy to keep some of my most-used spices in one of the levels (the rest of my less frequently used spices are in a cabinet), and when cooking just separate it from the unit and take it right to the stove. The smaller size with just the spices I need makes it easy to work with, and doesn't get in the way.

GETTING STARTED

As stressed in the introduction, so many of the projects you'll make on the following pages are used either with things you already have, or things you'll require for the completion of the project. Because what you'll use might not be the same as what I got, begin this project by measuring the spice containers you plan to use with this rack. (**PHOTO 1**)

I'm using a set of matching clear spice bottles for this rack, which measure 1¾" at the widest point and

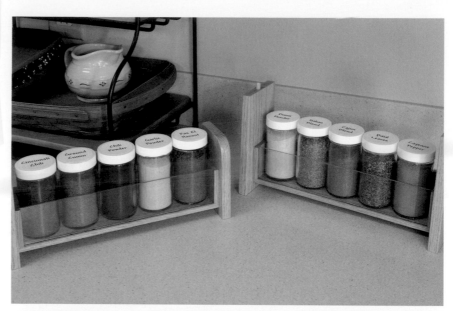

The first step of any project is to measure. Then, measure again.

stand 3¾" high, so all the parts and components for this project reflect that measurement. For your bottles, or if you choose to use the containers your spices came in, just measure them and alter dimensions accordingly. When measuring and adjusting your parts, be sure to allow a bit of extra wiggle room for the containers. For example, this spice rack holds five 1¾"-wide containers in a row – 8¾" total – but I've made the bottle holders with 9" inside, allowing an extra ¼" so they aren't jammed together in the rack.

Cut the bottle holder parts to width, but not length yet – we'll do

that after cutting the groove for the holder fronts of clear acrylic.

You can get clear acrylic at your local home center in various sizes, but you'll find the small 8" x 10" panels easiest to use. These sheets are a bit less than ⅛" thick, so either a standard or thin-kerf blade is fine for cutting the groove.

Measure and set your table saw fence to cut a groove ⅛" from the front edge of the workpiece for the holder sides and bottoms (they're the same width). Now, raise the blade to ⅛" and make the cut, as in **PHOTO 2**. Since this is a single extra-long workpiece you only need to make one

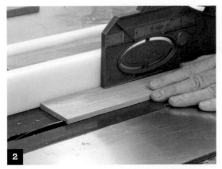
A single pass over the table saw creates the groove for the clear acrylic fronts.

Cut the holder sides to length. Note the magnetic stop I've used to repeat the cuts exactly.

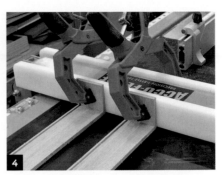
Begin the glue-up by attaching the bottle holder ends. Your table saw's rip fence makes a great square gluing jig.

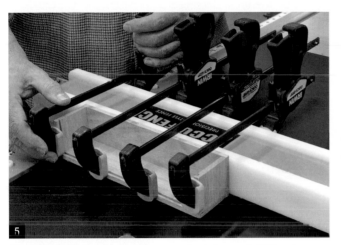
Attach the holder backs, clamping securely and squarely till the glue dries.

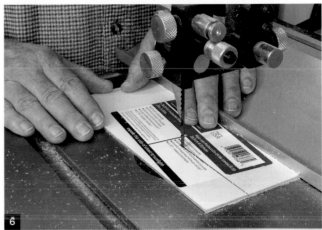
Cut the acrylic fronts to size. Leave the protective plastic film in place till the project is complete.

pass to cut the groove for all the parts needing it.

Cut your grooved workpiece to the appropriate length for the two bottom pieces and the four end pieces. In **PHOTO 3**, I've used a magnetic stop on the surface of my table saw to set the width of the parts – in this case, the holder ends – well ahead of the blade. With the miter gauge pulled back, register the workpiece against the stop and then push forward to make the cut. With the stop ahead of the blade, there's no danger of trapping the piece you've just cut between the stop and blade.

ASSEMBLE THE BOTTLE HOLDERS
Start assembly with the bottle holders. No complicated joinery here. We'll use simple butt joints, but everything will be plenty strong. First, this

spice rack is an extremely low-stress item – no heavy weight to bear and no shearing stresses in use – so the strength is already sufficient. Also, once the rack sides are added, those butt joints will become the equivalent of rabbet joints, increasing their strength even further.

Apply glue to the bottom edge of two holder ends and attach them on top of the holder bottoms at the end, as in **PHOTO 4**, making sure to line up the grooves on what will be the front of each holder. To keep things square I've clamped up these subassemblies using my table saw's rip fence as a clamping aid. The fence sides are perfectly perpendicular to the table, making it a great clamping jig. When the subassemblies have dried, flip them around and repeat on the opposite ends.

Now, apply glue around the three rear edges of each bottle holder and attach the backs, clamping up till dry as before. (**PHOTO 5**) The groove in the bottom will be visible on each end of the assembly now, but will be hidden later.

Measure and mark your acrylic sheets and cut them to size. This can be done on the band saw, as in **PHOTO 6**, as long as you're using a blade with a high tooth count. Your acrylic sheet will come with thin plastic film covering both sides to prevent scratching. Leave this film on as you work, and remove only after the project is completely done. Test fit the acrylic fronts into each holder and adjust the fit as needed, then sand the cut edges smooth with #150-grit or higher sandpaper. Put the acrylic fronts aside for now.

7

For uniformity, try to double-up identical parts like the spice rack sides and cut them simultaneously when possible.

8

Separate the two halves of the sides on the table saw. The length of these pieces corresponds to the height of the spice containers.

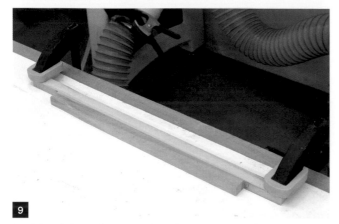

9

A quick jig helps to align parts when gluing the spice rack sides to the bottle holders.

10

Face-glue the sides of the bottom section to the holder ends, then repeat for the top section.

TAKING SIDES

Stack the two workpieces that will become the sides atop each other, then secure together with painter's tape. These two side pieces are identical, and whenever cutting identical parts I like to stack or otherwise group them together and cut them simultaneously, ensuring that each subsequent part is the same. Another plus is you only have to copy patterns or mark cutlines once. You'll see this trick used several times throughout the book.

By the way, although the completed spice rack sides measure 3⅛" x 10½", I like to use a slightly oversized workpiece to cut them out. At 3⅛" wide and ½" thick, a standard piece of ½" x 4" oak (which really measures only 3½" wide) was a good choice.

Using the Spice Rack Side View guide on page 17, mark the cut line for the rack front edge, then cut on your mark. (**PHOTO 7**)

With the workpieces still taped together, mark and cut the upper and lower halves of the spice rack sides to length, as in **PHOTO 8**. Be sure to take your saw's kerf into consideration to get a combined height of 10½" when the two are stacked vertically later.

Remove the painter's tape to separate the individual sides, taking care to keep each side together as a unit (this ensures that the grain is continuous on each side of the completed rack).

Each half of the sides extends ½" below the bottle holders. To make it easy to set this distance, as well as to act as a squaring guide, make a quick

assembly jig like the one shown in **PHOTO 9**. This is simply a ½" x ½" strip of scrap cut to the exact length of the holder (9½"), glued to another strip of scrap long enough to clamp to my workbench.

To assemble each section, apply glue to the ends of the lower bottle holder and align it on the front of the assembly jig. Now, sandwich the holder in between the two side pieces for the lower section, and clamp up till dry. (**PHOTO 10**) Repeat with the upper section.

STACK THE RACK

To secure the two sections when stacked, add alignment pins to the tops of the bottom section. These are just short lengths of ¼" dowel that mate the two sections.

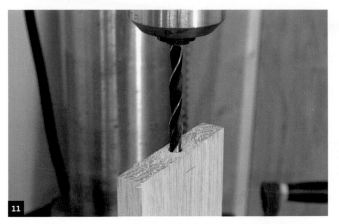

11

12

Center ¼" holes in the tops of the bottom section for the alignment pins.

Use dowel centers to mark the underside of the top section for perfect alignment.

Center and drill a ¼" hole ⅜" deep into the tops of the lower rack section. These should be perfectly vertical, so a drill press works best here. (**PHOTO 11**)

To match these holes to the underside of the upper section, slip ¼" dowel centers (sometimes called dowel points) into the holes. Lay the upper and lower sections on their backs and align against a square edge – the table saw fence is perfect for this – and press the two pieces together. In **PHOTO 12**, you can see how the dowel center has created a dimple on the opposing piece exactly where the corresponding hole goes. Now, just turn the upper section upside down and drill ¼" holes on the marks, also ⅜" deep.

By the way, in **PHOTO 12** you can see how those butt joints used to create the bottle holder effectively become rabbet joints when the sides are attached. Where before there was just a single glue joint – the original butt joint – there are now two glue joints at right angles.

Cut two ¾" lengths of ¼" hardwood dowel, and glue one into each of the holes in the lower section. When stacked, the upper section fits right over those two alignment pins for a uniform appearance.

Mark and cut the curves on the front of the upper section per the Side View guide. I cut the corners

13

A disc sander quickly rounds off the front edge of the top section sides.

with a jigsaw, and then smoothed the curve with a disc sander. (**PHOTO 13**) I waited till now to cut this curve so the top would be full width, making it easier to set squarely upside down for drilling the dowel holes on the underside.

Finally, peel the film from the acrylic fronts and slip them into place in their grooves.

NOW, MAKE IT YOUR OWN

You can customize your spice rack any number of ways. I made this one for my 10 most-used spices, so the first thing you might consider is altering the dimensions to accommodate as many spice containers of any size you like. This one handles those glass bottles you see in the lead photo,

which measure 3¾", and the opening between the lower and upper holders is such that the bottles can easily be tilted forward and removed from the lower section. When adjusting size, be sure you allow this tilting room for removing the containers.

I made this rack of oak, but any wood you want to use is fine, although I find the stacked unit to be more stable with a heavier hardwood. There are no food-contact issues, so open- or closed-grain woods are equally suitable.

This spice rack received two coats of satin polyurethane, but use whatever finish is your favorite. Also, feel free to stain the wood – or even mix wood species of different shades – to suit your tastes.

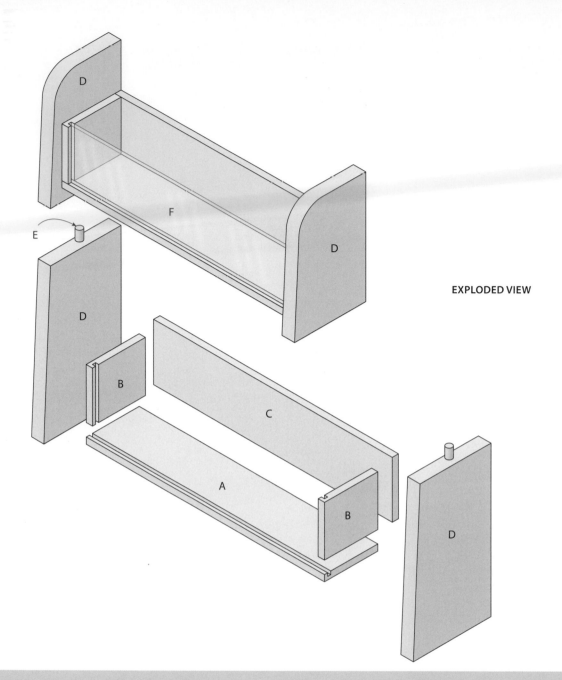

EXPLODED VIEW

MODULAR SPICE RACK CUT LIST

Overall Dimensions: 3⅛" deep x 10½" wide x 10½" tall

REF	QTY	PART	STOCK	THICKNESS	WIDTH	LENGTH
A	2	Bottle Holder Bottoms	Oak	¼"	2⅛"	9½"
B	4	Bottle Holder Ends	Oak	¼"	2⅛"	2"
C	2	Bottle Holder Backs	Oak	¼"	2¼"	9½"
D	2	Spice Rack Side	Oak	½"	3⅛"	10½" (a)
E	2	Alignment Pins	Hardwood Dowel	¼"	n/a"	¾"
F	2	Bottle Holder Fronts	Clear Acrylic	⅛" (b)	2⅛"	9¼"

NOTES:

(a) Dimension is finished size of combined two-piece side. Make workpiece slightly larger to allow for cutting and shaping.

(b) Thickness approximate; actual thickness is slightly less.

ADDITIONAL MATERIALS:

Thin acrylic (Plexiglas, Lexan, etc.) for holder front

Optional – Matching Spice Bottles (10 needed)

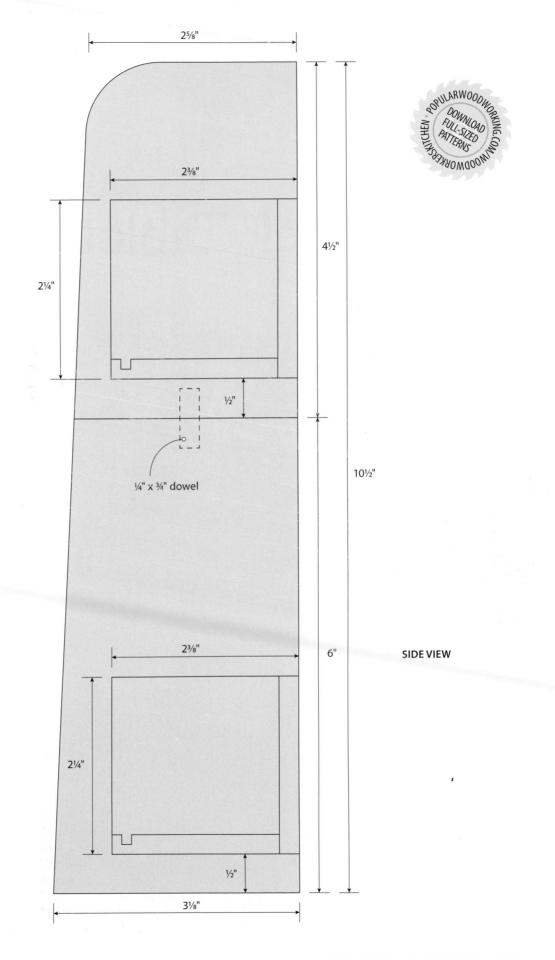

2⅝"

2⅜"

4½"

2¼"

½"

¼" x ¾" dowel

10½"

6"

SIDE VIEW

2⅜"

2¼"

½"

3⅛"

Knife Block Tablet Holder

EVERY KITCHEN NEEDS A PLACE to keep knives. If your kitchen's like mine, you have dozens of knives of several types and sizes squirreled away everywhere. Chances are good you've grouped them by type – table knives with the silverware, meal prep knives where you work, and the "knives for when we have company" in a nice case in the dining room. But you want the knives you use every day close by, and a knife block on a kitchen counter makes them available at arm's reach. (And, frankly, a kitchen without a knife block as part of the decor just doesn't seem right.)

You can buy a knife block, of course, but then you have someone else's idea of what knives belong in it. Wouldn't it be nicer to design your own, based on the knives you have and use most often? Of course it would.

My favorite TV chef, Alton Brown on the Food Network, loves kitchen tools but hates things that serve only one purpose. He calls these single-use items "uni-taskers," and always prefers efficient kitchen gear that does more than one thing. I couldn't agree more, so the knife block in this project serves two purposes. Not only is it home to your favorite cutlery, but it also incorporates a small shelf that serves as a stand for a tablet or smart phone. Angled for perfect viewing, this tablet holder allows you to bring up a favorite recipe or stream a cooking show while you work.

AROUND THE BLOCK

The heart of this project is a pair of core blocks where all the slots are cut. Laminated to size from thinner workpieces, they form the inner portion of the knife block. These core blocks receive trim pieces on the sides that either close the slots or hide the glue joints from the lamination process (or both).

Start with the main core block by cutting the lamination workpieces to size. (**PHOTO 1**) You'll want to trim the sides of the completed glue-up, so make each of the workpieces just a

Cut the workpieces for the main core block to size.

Spread glue on the workpiece faces, then stack and clamp.

Dress the block sides on the jointer – these faces are where the slots are cut.

Before cutting the slots, measure your knives for a custom fit.

Set the table saw fence and blade for each cut, then run the block through.

bit wider than listed in the Cut List.

Spread glue on the inner faces of the workpieces, as in **PHOTO 2**, then clamp up the assembly.

When the main core block is dry, dress the side faces as needed on the jointer. (**PHOTO 3**) You'll shave off a bit of width here, which is why we made the workpieces slightly wider than the finished core block width of 4½".

As always when making something specifically for your own kitchen tools, a key first step is measuring the knives you want to store. (**PHOTO 4**) First mark one end of the core block for the knife locations, making sure to take the handle thickness into account for spacing. Most knife blades are really thin – ⅟₁₆" or less – but trying to insert knives into slots that small is more difficult than it should be, so plan on slots of at least ⅛" or, even better, ³⁄₁₆" as I've used here.

Now, measure the blades at their widest points, and add a bit more – ³⁄₁₆" to ¼" extra is good.

Head back to the table saw and raise the blade height to match the knife width for the first slot, set and lock the fence to cut on your first mark, then cut through the entire length of the block, as in **PHOTO 5**. With a standard-kerf blade (⅛"), re-setting the fence by ⅟₁₆" and making another pass gives you a ³⁄₁₆" slot.

Reset the blade height and fence for the next slot, cut, and repeat until all the slots on one side are done. Now, flip the block over and do the other side.

For the wider slots for the sharpening steel and kitchen shears, I just made repeated passes and reset the fence to get the ½" and ¾" slots I needed. However, if you prefer you can cut these wider slots in a single pass with a dado blade in your table saw or on a router table outfitted with a straight bit.

Apply glue to the sides of the core block and clamp the side pieces into place. (**PHOTO 6**) This effectively closes the slots on the interior of the block. It also hides the lamination on the block sides with an unbroken surface of continuous grain.

A SOLID BASE

Making the base core block is pretty much the same process. Because the base is basically a short triangle,

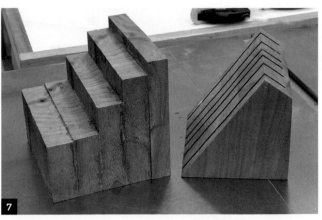

Glue the block sides in place to close the slots and hide the lamination joints.

At left is a fresh glue-up for the base core block; at right, a finished base ready to go.

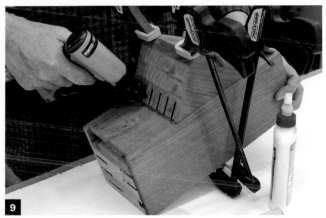

Cut the base core block to shape on the band saw.

A few pin nails driven from the underside keep the base block from shifting while clamped.

I conserved wood by gluing it up mostly of scraps with a nicely figured piece on the front. As you can see in **PHOTO 7**, I only needed to use pieces long enough to create the triangle shape. Cut your pieces to width, then glue and clamp up the block as before.

When the base core block is dry, dress the sides as before for a smooth gluing surface. Now, mark the base angle according to the Base Profile Pattern on page 23. Make sure you've taken the grain direction into account, and cut the base to shape on the band saw. (**PHOTO 8**)

Cut the two base sides using the Base Profile Pattern, and glue and clamp them to the base core block. When dry, trim and sand as needed to complete the triangular base. You'll

note that I've oriented the grain on the base sides so it's vertical in the finished knife block, but if you prefer you can cut them out with the grain aligned in the same direction as the grain in the base. Each has a unique look, so pick the one you like best.

Sand the base's cut face smooth, and cut knife slots into that face on the table saw per the Steak Knife Slot Pattern on page 24. Of course, you can cut the slots to accommodate any desired cutlery.

Apply glue to the slotted face of the base and affix it to the underside of the main block 8¼" from the top edge per the Main Block Profile on page 24. The base is slightly narrower than the main block, so center it left-to-right to create a small reveal on each side. Clamp the assembly light-

ly, just enough to hold steady. This is a weird set of clamping angles, likely to move things around once full pressure is applied, so I opted to give it a helping hand by shooting a couple of pin nails into the assembly from the underside of the base and into the main block, as in **PHOTO 9**. A pair of nails is all you need to keep things from sliding around. With the base secured, fully tighten the clamps and allow the assembly to dry.

Use a ruler to pencil a mark in line with the base bottom across the main block, then cut off the main block at the same angle. (**PHOTO 10**) Now measure ¾" up from the bottom of the main block front and make a second cut squarely across for the tablet shelf.

The shelf assembly is simply a

right angle created from the ¼"-thick shelf piece and a ⅜"-thick shelf front, as noted on the Shelf Profile drawing on page 25. Cut and glue the two pieces together, and when dry, glue and clamp it to the bottom front edge of the main block, as in **PHOTO 11**. When this has dried, trim the back edge of the shelf flush with the underside of the knife block.

Finish the completed knife block any way you like, but a polyurethane varnish provides the best protection against scratches and potential cooking splatters. Finally, add some peel-off adhesive felt glides to the underside of the block. The felt will allow you to slide the block around on your countertop or rotate it to make both the knife and tablet sides of the block accessible.

10 Cut the bottom angle of the main block to match that of the base block.

11 Glue and clamp the shelf assembly to the foot of the completed knife block.

POPULARWOODWORKING.COM/WOODWORKERSKITCHEN
DOWNLOAD FULL-SIZED PATTERNS

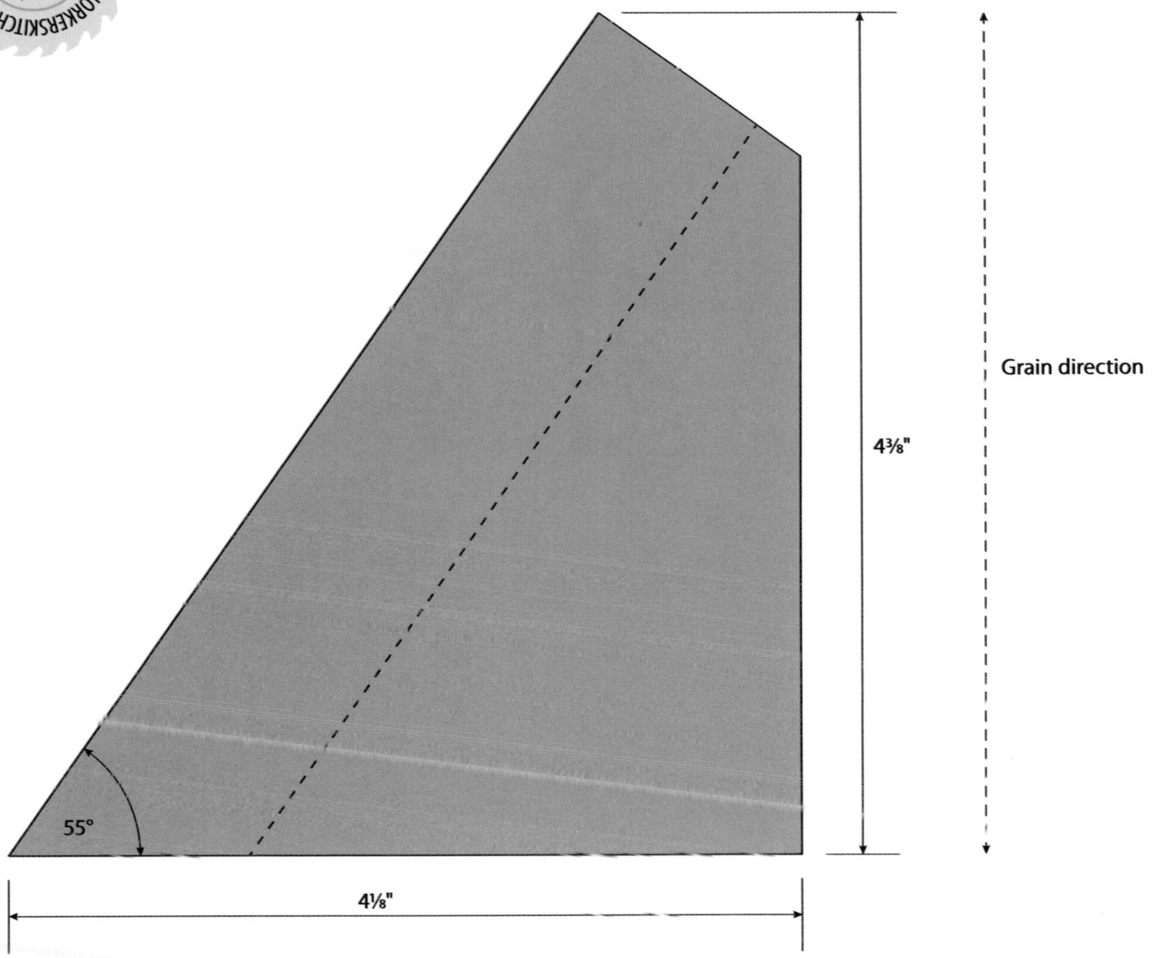

4⅜"
Grain direction
55°
4⅛"

BASE PROFILE PATTERN

KNIFE BLOCK CUT LIST

Overall Dimensions: 11⅔" deep x 5¼" wide x 9¼" tall

QTY	PART	STOCK	THICKNESS	WIDTH	LENGTH
1	Main Core Block	Walnut	4½"	4¾"	12" (a)
2	Main Core Block Sides	Walnut	⅜"	4¾"	12"
1	Base Core Block	Walnut	4⅛"	4⅝"	4⅜" (a)
2	Base Core Block Sides	Walnut	⅛"	4⅛"	4⅜"
1	Tablet Shelf	Walnut	¼"	1¾"	5¼"
1	Shelf Front	Walnut	⅜"	½"	5¼"

NOTES:

(a) Final dimensions of unshaped workpiece, laminated of thinner pieces

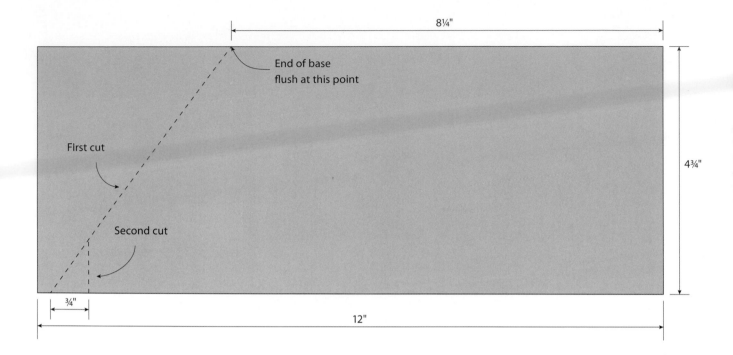

MAIN BLOCK PROFILE

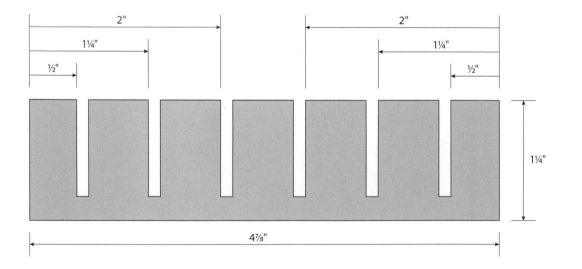

STEAK KNIFE SLOT PATTERN

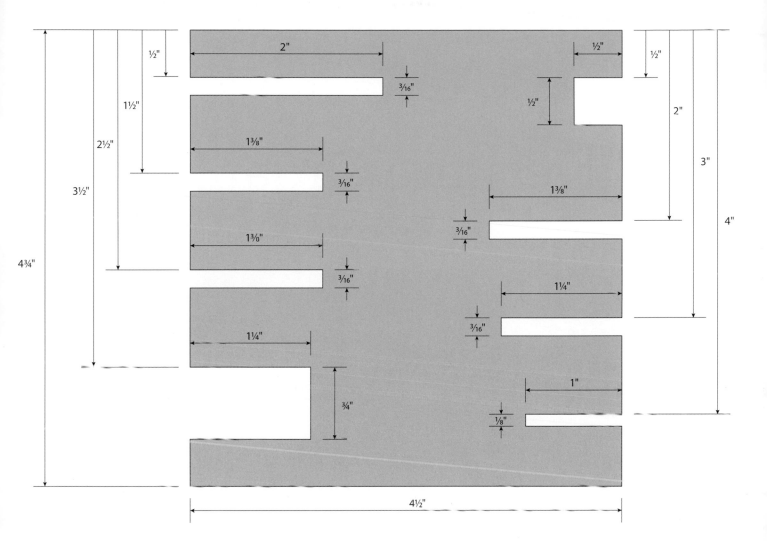

MAIN CORE BLOCK SLOT PATTERN

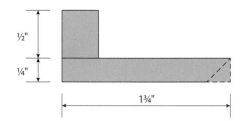

SHELF PROFILE

Silverware Organizer

YOU PROBABLY HAVE SOME kind of organizer tray inside a kitchen drawer for silverware or other utensils, and chances are good it's made of thin injection-molded plastic. Nothing wrong with these as long as you leave them in the drawer, but pull one out fully loaded with silverware and it'll flex and bend under the weight. It's also not that easy to get in and out, as you have to dig around the edges to get your fingers underneath of it.

Wouldn't it be better if the organizer had a handle to make carrying it easier, and if it was made of something strong enough that it didn't flop around all over the place when trying to carry it? I designed this one to address both deficiencies of generic plastic silverware organizers.

Made of sturdy ⅜" maple with a centered handle for balance, this organizer fits inside most kitchen drawers – handle and all – and is easily removed and returned to the drawer whenever you want. Another plus, you can build one custom-sized specifically for your drawers, with dividers designed and arranged just the way you want them.

PREP THE PARTS

Cut all the parts to width – 2¼" for the front/back pieces and sides, 1¾" for the front and side dividers, and 3" for the handle divider. Also cut them to the approximate lengths from the Cut List, allowing some extra length on each piece. We'll trim them to the exact length later.

The organizer sides and ends receive a ¼" groove for the plywood bottom, and we'll cut that with a ¼" dado blade set on the table saw. If you prefer, you can use a ¼" straight bit in a router table. Set your fence so the blade is ¼" from the bottom edge of the workpiece, then raise the blade to ³⁄₁₆". With everything set, run the front, back and both sides through to cut the grooves. (**PHOTO 1**)

To make any box perfectly square, the opposite sides must exactly match each other in length. As we've done

Create the groove for the plywood bottom with a ¼" dado cutter on the table saw.

With the corresponding sides stacked, cut them to length simultaneously for exactly matching pairs.

Cut ⅜"-wide rabbets ³⁄₁₆" deep on each end of the organizer sides.

before, I like to tape these pairs and cut them simultaneously to turn out perfect sets of parts. Stack the sides atop each other, then tape them together. Now, cut them to length. (**PHOTO 2**) The two ends and the front divider are also the same length, so stack them and cut all three at the same time too.

Cut ⅜" rabbets ³⁄₁₆" deep on each end of the two sides. In **PHOTO 3**, I'm doing this with a dado blade set on the table saw, but you can also use a straight bit in a router table.

The sides also receive dados for a divider that creates a short storage compartment at the front. (**PHOTO 4**) No need to change the blade height, just the fence position. Once I decided which end of the two sides

belonged in front, I butted their edges together and taped them to keep them straight, and then cut the opposing dados for the divider in a single pass.

With the blade still at ³⁄₁₆", cut the dados on the inner faces of the back piece and front divider for the three center dividers – actually, two side dividers and the center handle divider. Same as before, I butted them together and taped them, then milled three dados, one in the center and the other two even spaced on either side.

This is a good time to do a dry assembly to check everything out. The front/back pieces and the front divider were cut as a set, so everything should be true and square. However, before cutting the three remaining

With the two sides taped together, cut the ⅜" dados for the front divider.

Clamp up a dry assembly of the organizer, and measure for the exact length of the side and handle dividers.

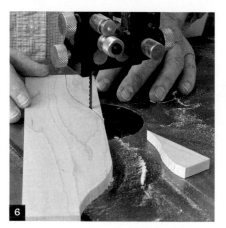

Cut the handle profile on the band saw, as shown here, or with a jigsaw or scrollsaw.

Define the handle opening by drilling a 1¼" hole on each end.

Use a jigsaw to connect the two holes and complete the handle opening.

dividers to length it's best to get an exact measurement, as in **PHOTO 5**. Cut all three to length, and put the two side dividers aside while we concentrate on the handle divider.

Transfer the Handle Pattern from page 30 to the center divider workpiece, then cut the shape out. I'm using the band saw in **PHOTO 6**, but you can also use a jigsaw or scrollsaw.

Start the handle opening by first drilling a 1¼" hole at each end with a Forstner bit. (**PHOTO 7**) With both holes drilled, cut between the two holes to create the handle opening, as in **PHOTO 8**. I've sized this opening so my large hands fit easily, but if you have smaller hands you can make the opening less than 1¼".

Before assembly, give the inner surfaces of all the parts a good sand-ing up to #150-grit, or #220 if you like things really smooth. (**PHOTO 9**) It's a lot easier to sand these inner surfaces now, especially where the dadoed parts go together, than after the assembly is glued up.

The last part of prepping the parts is to cut the plywood bottom to size. As with the other parts, sand the inner surface smooth.

TAKING SHAPE

Dry assemble everything again, this time with the plywood bottom in place but with the intended inner surface facing down. Why? Well, these organizers hold a lot of weight, and to keep the bottom from sagging we'll reinforce it. We could just glue those dividers at the bottom, but I prefer the extra strength afforded by screws

driven up from underneath and into the dividers. To place the screw locations, mark the outside edge of those dividers in pencil, as in **PHOTO 10**. No need to trace the entire length, just small marks on each side of the divider where the screws will go. Mark the side dividers in the middle of their length, while the center handle divider gets two marks for screws on each side of handle opening.

There are 12 dado/rabbet joints, rather difficult to juggle trying to do them all at once, so we'll do the glue-up in steps. Start by gluing the front piece and front divider into their respective rabbets/dados. Then put the back piece in place dry – no glue! – to square the assembly and then clamp up. (**PHOTO 11**) Check for square and allow to dry.

9

Before final assembly, give all inside surfaces a good sanding.

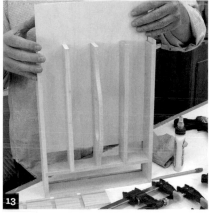

10

Do one more dry assembly and slip the side and handle dividers in place to mark where they meet the bottom.

11

Begin the assembly by gluing the organizer front and front divider into place. There's no glue on the back piece yet, but it keeps the assembly square till the front is dry.

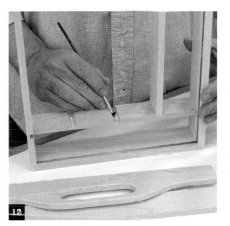

12

Apply glue into the dados on the front divider, then slip the side and handle dividers into place.

13

Slide the organizer bottom into its slots, then glue the back piece into place and clamp up till dry.

14

Using the marks you made earlier, countersink and drive ¾" screws into the dividers from underneath.

Next, apply glue in the dados on the inner surface of the front divider, as in **PHOTO 12**, and put each divider in place. The two side dividers can go in either way, but the center divider should be oriented with the handle centered in the assembly. Put the back piece in place, again with no glue, check for square, and clamp up till dry.

When dry, remove the clamps and slip the plywood bottom in place with the inner surface facing upward, as in **PHOTO 13**. Your drilling marks will now be on the underside of the assembly. Apply glue into the dados and rabbets on the back end piece, and then clamp everything up one last time to complete the assembly.

When dry, support the organizer upside down – I'm using a couple 2x4 offcuts to raise the handle off my worktable – and drill countersunk holes between your marks and up into the dividers. Now, drive in four ¾" flat-head screws to secure the plywood bottom to the dividers from underneath. (**PHOTO 14**)

FINISHING THOUGHTS

Sand the outside of the completed organizer, and add the finish of your choice. This will take a beating from the silverware, especially on the inside, so a few coats of polyurethane will give the most protection from scrapes and scratches.

I've geared this organizer to fit my kitchen silverware drawer for size and handle height, but measure your drawer and adjust dimensions as needed. Likewise, rearrange and resize the dividers and sections any way you like. You can even make multiples – one for silverware in one drawer, one for utensils in another. If you entertain a lot, consider making one solely for toting things around.

You can use any wood you want for your organizer, but I'd stick with hardwood for strength and stability. This isn't a food-contact item so any hardwood you like is fine.

By the way, with a few tweaks an organizer like this isn't restricted to the kitchen. I made a couple very similar to this one that I use as tool totes in my workshop.

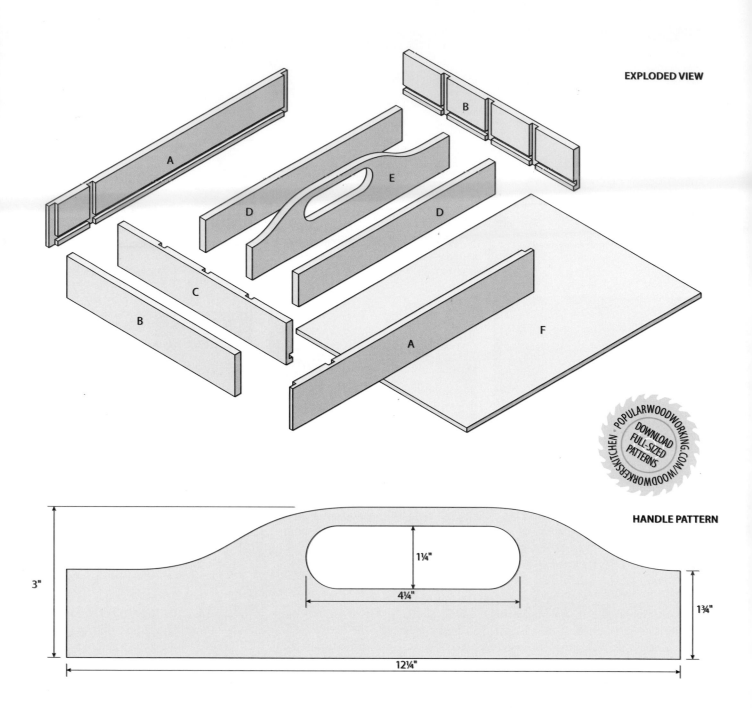

HANDLE PATTERN

3"

1¼"

4¼"

1¾"

12¼"

SILVERWARE ORGANIZER CUT LIST

Overall Dimensions: 3½" x 11" x 15" (including handle height)

REF	QTY	PART	STOCK	THICKNESS	WIDTH	LENGTH
A	2	Sides	Maple	⅜"	2¼"	15"
B	2	Front/Back	Maple	⅜"	2¼"	10⅝"
C	1	Front Divider	Maple	⅜"	1¾"	10⅝"
D	2	Side Dividers	Maple	⅜"	1¾"	12¼"
E	1	Handle Divider	Maple	⅜"	3"	12¼"
F	1	Bottom	Birch Plywood	¼"	10⅝"	14⅝"

K-Cup Brewing Center

THERE'S NOT A MORNING IN our house where there isn't at least one full pot of coffee on our drip brewer, but once in a while you just want a single cup.

The people at Keurig Green Mountain created a popular niche in kitchen appliances when they developed K-Cup brewers for commercial use in 1998, followed by the first home brewers in 2004. Using a single-serve pod dubbed the K-Cup, a really good single cup of coffee was now within reach for anyone, anytime. Since then, other manufacturers have introduced their own brewers, with K-Cups available for virtually any brand of coffee you could want.

You can store your K-Cups anywhere, of course, but a stand incorporating a storage drawer keeps everything together. The all-wood unit presented here would be an attractive addition to any kitchen.

The brewing center base is walnut, while the drawer underneath is of poplar construction with a drawer front of nicely figured cherry highlighted with a walnut pull. The drawer is sized for five rows of six K-Cups each. Of course, you can use your favorite hardwood and you can change the dimensions as you wish to increase or decrease the platform size and amount of storage.

This isn't a self-contained cabinet in the usual sense, but rather a storage box with a fitted cover – think of the drawer nestled in the base like a car parked in a garage. Not only does this keep construction simpler, but it also helps reduce the overall height for clearance under a kitchen cabinet.

Speaking of construction, we'll use rabbet and groove joinery for the drawer. The base, meanwhile, will be simple butt joints.

MEASURE FIRST

My maker is a Keurig 2.0 with a 9" x 12" footprint, so all project dimensions are based on that. A smaller machine works fine with these dimensions, but if your machine is bigger then you'll need to enlarge yours.

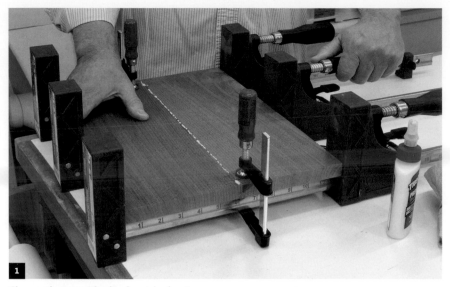

Glue up the top with a bookmatched pattern.

Drawer capacity is determined by the size of the K-Cups. Although the drawer height needs to accommodate the 1¾"-high pods no matter how many it contains, the width and length are determined by the 2"-wide K-Cups, so your drawer interior will be multiples of 2", plus a little extra so the cups aren't jammed together. For five rows of six cups, I took the basic internal capacity of 10" x 12", then added ¼".

The final dimension to consider is the total height once the brewer is atop the base platform. With the material used and the K-Cup height, the brewing center comes in at 3⅛" high. Add the height of the brewer, and be sure everything fits underneath your cabinets. Standard kitchen cabinet height today is 18" above the countertop, but some newer homes are going with deeper cabinets set at a slightly higher 21". Meanwhile, 15" was a common height not too many years ago, and the cabinet height in really old homes could be anything at all so, as always, measure.

Depending on your machine's design and your cabinet clearance, you may need to slide the unit forward to raise the brewer's access lid. Stick-on felt glide discs attached to the underside of the base make this easy.

COFFEE DRAWER

We'll construct the base in the next part, but go ahead and glue up the base platform so it can be drying in the clamps while making the drawer. For the platform I oriented the grain front-to-back, and for a uniform look with the end grain on the front I cut a long workpiece and folded it back on itself to create a bookmatched panel, and then glued it up. (**PHOTO 1**)

Cut the drawer sides and front/back to width on the table saw, as in **PHOTO 2**, then crosscut them to length. As in earlier projects, I cut the sides and the front/back to length as pairs to ensure they matched exactly.

Poplar's a great secondary wood for drawer boxes, but consider using a wood species for the drawer front that compliments the walnut base. I had a thin piece of figured cherry I've been dying to use, but it was only ⅛" and so I laminated it to some poplar to create the ⅜"-thick front. Of course, you'll find it easier to cut the front from solid ⅜" material.

Cut ⅜"-wide rabbets ³⁄₁₆" deep in each end of the drawer front and back. In **PHOTO 3**, I'm using a ⅜" dado blade set on the table saw, but a straight bit in a router table also works well. I've taped the two pieces

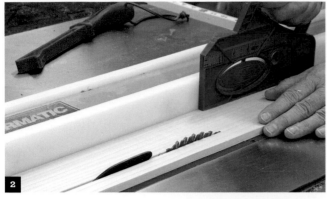

Cut the drawer sides to width on the table saw, then cut the parts to length.

The drawer front and back get a ⅜"-wide rabbet on each end.

A standard-kerf saw blade creates the ⅛" slot for the drawer's plywood bottom.

Glue the drawer front into place, check for square, and clamp up till dry.

together to cut the rabbets in both pieces at the same time.

The drawer bottom is ⅛" plywood – the drawer only holds a few ounces of K-Cups, so no need for anything stronger. A standard-kerf blade on the table saw is perfectly sized for the grooves. Set the fence so the blade is ⅛" from the bottom edge of the drawer components, then raise the blade to ³⁄₁₆" and run all four workpieces through. (**PHOTO 4**)

Cut the drawer bottom to size and then give the inside faces of all the parts a thorough sanding up to #150- or #220-grit. (It's easier now than after the glue-up.)

Assemble the drawer in two steps, starting at either end. Apply glue in the rabbets on one end and fit the sides into place, aligning the groves.

To keep the assembly square, put the other end in place without glue, and clamp up. (**PHOTO 5**) Check for square and adjust as needed.

When dry, remove the clamps and slide the drawer bottom into place. (**PHOTO 6**) Now, add glue to the remaining rabbets, fit the opposite end into place, check for square and clamp up till dry.

With a capacity of 30 K-Cups, let's keep the inside of the drawer organized by adding some low dividers to separate the rows and keep the cups from sliding around. These don't need to be very high and they certainly don't need to be fancy. Four ⅜" x ⅜" strips of poplar evenly spaced and glued right to the drawer's plywood bottom will work perfectly. (**PHOTO 7**)

A SOLID BASE

Remove the base platform glue-up from the clamps. Since the width of platform determines the width of the drawer opening, before cutting it to size measure the completed drawer to verify the width, then add ⅛" for side clearance. The length of the platform, meanwhile, equals the length of the drawer plus the ¾" base back. With these measurements confirmed, cut the platform to size.

Now, cut the base back to size with the grain running across the narrower dimension. The reason for this is that we're using a simple butt joint to attach the back, so we want any seasonal width variation to be consistent between the base platform and back. Apply glue to the mating edge of the base back, and clamp it

Slide in the drawer bottom, then glue and clamp the drawer back to complete the assembly.

Glue evenly spaced ⅜" x ⅜" dividers onto the drawer bottom.

Glue and clamp the base back into place. Note that the grain runs the same direction as the base platform.

to the underside of the base platform at the back edge. (**PHOTO 8**)

Cut the base sides to size and glue and clamp them to sides of the base assembly. Again, these are butt joints, but the major joints on both sides of the base are long-grain to long-grain and plenty strong. By the way, the sides are cut from a longer piece so the crosscut ends facing forward are also bookmatched.

When everything's dry, tilt your table saw's blade to 5° to bevel the sides. With the base upside down on the saw table, set the fence so the blade cleanly slices off just enough stock to angle the sides, as in **PHOTO 9**. With both sides cut, the base is ready for sanding.

The last step is to add a pull to the coffee drawer. I opted for a wooden pull of walnut to match the base. This is simply a small piece of walnut centered and face-glued to the front of the drawer and clamped into place till dry. (**PHOTO 10**)

For final finishing, keep in mind that the brewing center is going to be used with and exposed to water frequently, so polyurethane is your best choice.

Tilt the table saw blade to 5° and with the assembly upside down, cut the stand's beveled sides.

Glue and clamp the drawer pull to the center of the drawer front.

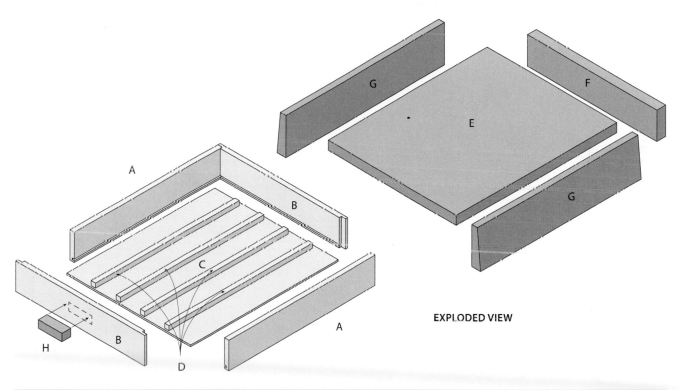

EXPLODED VIEW

K-CUP BREWING CENTER CUT LIST

Overall Dimensions: 3⅛" x 12⅝" x 13¾"

REF	QTY	PART	STOCK	THICKNESS	WIDTH	LENGTH
A	2	Drawer Sides	Poplar	⅜"	2¼"	12⅝"
B	2	Drawer Back/Front	Poplar (a)	⅜"	2¼"	11"
C	1	Drawer Bottom	Birch Plywood	⅛"	10⅝"	12⅝"
D	4	Drawer Divider Strips	Poplar	⅜"	⅜"	12¼"
E	1	Base Platform	Walnut	¾"	11⅛"	13¾"
F	1	Base Back	Walnut	¾"	2⅜"	11⅛"
G	2	Base Sides	Walnut	¾"	3⅛"	13¾"
H	1	Drawer Pull	Walnut	⅝"	¾"	2"

NOTES:

(a) The drawer front can be made of any attractive hardwood; the project drawer has a thin false front of figured cherry, laminated to a poplar back for a total thickness of ⅜".

Utility Holder

I ORIGINALLY MADE THE FIRST of these holders many years ago. It was made from cherry and sized specifically to hold coffee filters. It looked so nice that we just left it out all the time near our coffee pot.

A few years later I made another in a different wood species for a new look, but instead of giving the old one away I simply used it to hold something else that fit. That's when it occurred to me that although I had only been thinking of coffee filters in the beginning, these little holders are adaptable to a variety of tasks in the kitchen (and everywhere else around the house, for that matter) – all you need to do is change a few key dimensions. Because they're small, these are also great projects to consider when you want to put some of your shop scrap to work. They're so ridiculously fast and easy to make, you can readily turn out several at a time. Finally, if you have small children you'd like to introduce to woodworking these can be a perfect first project for them – though you'll want to handle some of the cutting chores yourself.

We'll take a look at two sizes of these holders in this chapter, but you can make them any size at all and adjust the capacity to suit whatever your needs may be. I'll make a larger one sized for #4 coffee filters from pine, and a smaller one for #2 filters in walnut. True to form, both the pine and walnut came from my scrap barrel.

MAKING MULTIPLES

Cut the side pieces to width on the table saw. (**PHOTO 1**) I'm not worrying at all about length at this point; rather, I'm just churning out enough to make a few of these at once.

Cut the front/back pieces to size. Again, as you can see in **PHOTO 2**, I've got enough stock to make a number of these components. We'll be working with these as rectangles for now, but we'll shape them later.

Locate the center of a front piece and drill a hole through it with a

1 Cut the side workpieces to width on the table saw.

2 Cut the holder front and back pieces.

3 Center and drill a 1⅝" hole in the front workpiece.

Forstner bit. (**PHOTO 3**) For the larger pine holder I'm drilling a 1⅝" hole; for the smaller walnut one, a 1⅜" hole. I'm only drilling the hole in the fronts of these holders, by the way, because I like the look, but there's no reason you can't drill both front and back if you'd like. Or not drill a hole at all, for that matter.

Cut the two side pieces and the shorter bottom piece to length, and glue them to the inside edges of a back piece. Now, spread more glue on the upper part of the sides and top with the holder front. (**PHOTO 4**)

Clamp up everything until dry.

(**PHOTO 5**) Scrape or wipe off any glue squeeze-out from the outside of the assembly. For any squeeze-out that occurs on the inside, allow the glue to set a bit till it's thickened to a rubbery consistency, and then use a chisel, putty knife, or even a long narrow piece of square-ended scrap to scrape any glue out of the inner corners.

When the glue has cured, pencil an arc at the top from one side to the other. Likewise, mark the bottom corners round. You can do these with a compass, but you probably have something handy you can trace

4

Apply glue to the side pieces and sandwich them between the front/back pieces.

5

Clamp up the assembly till dry.

6

Shape the holder top and lower corners on the band saw.

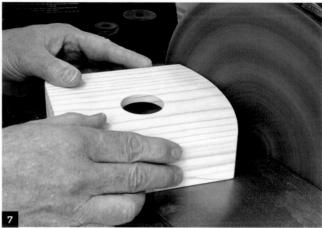

7

A disc sander is ideal for smoothing all curved surfaces·

around. I did the wide top arc with a dinner platter, and the corners simply by reaching into my pocket, pulling out a dime, and tracing around it.

Cut the top arc and the corners on the band saw. (**PHOTO 6**)

Sand off any saw marks on the corners and top arcs with a sanding block or orbital sander. If you have a disc sander, it's ideal for curved sanding. (**PHOTO 7**)

That's it. The holder is now complete. All that remains is to give it the finish of your choice, and I went with polyurethane to protect it from the occasional splashes it's sure to receive on my kitchen countertop.

I used ⅜"- and ½"-thick stock for the larger holder in these photos, while the smaller one in the opening photograph uses ⅜" walnut for the back and sides and ⅛" walnut for the front. These are the stock thicknesses reflected in the Cut List with the project, but don't confine yourself to these dimensions. Likewise, while I made these to fit #4 and #2 coffee filters, make them larger or smaller as you see fit. If you have thicker items you want rounded up in an attractive holder like this, increase the depth from front to back by using wider side pieces.

Also, instead of a hole in the cen-

ter you could cut a vertical slot that would make it easy to retrieve shorter items stored in one of these. Rather than a convex curve on the top, consider a concave one or none at all. If you'd like a holder that hangs on a wall or inside a cupboard, leave the front piece as is but lengthen the back piece and add a hanging hole at the top. And if it hangs, no need for a square base.

The customization possibilities really are endless.

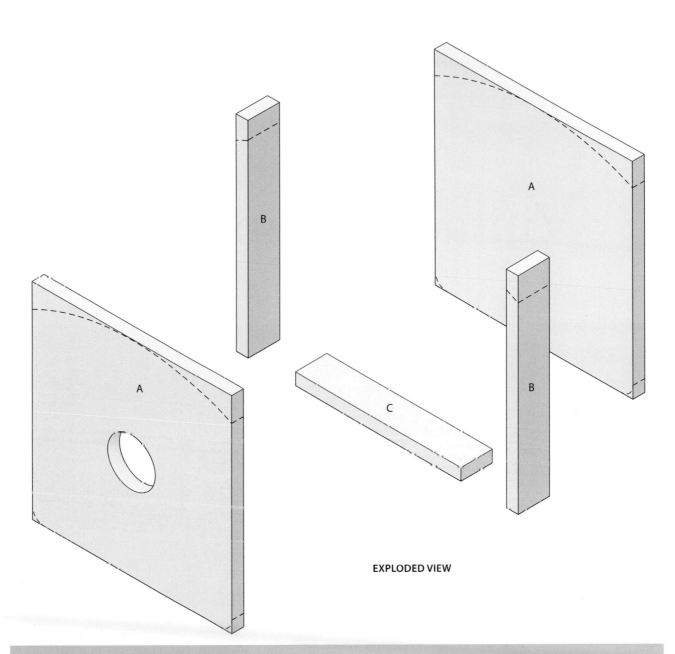

EXPLODED VIEW

UTILITY HOLDER CUT LIST

Overall Dimensions: Large – 1¾" deep x 6¼" wide x 6½" tall; Small – 1¼" deep x 5⅛" wide x 4½" tall

REF	QTY	PART	STOCK	THICKNESS	WIDTH	LENGTH
LARGE (#4 COFFEE FILTER)						
A	2	Front/Back	Pine	⅜"	6¼"	6½"
B	2	Sides	Pine	½"	1"	6½" (a)
C	1	Bottom	Pine	½"	1"	5¼"
SMALL (#2 COFFEE FILTER) (b)						
	1	Front	Walnut	⅛"	5⅛"	4½"
	1	Back	Walnut	⅜"	5⅛"	4½"
	2	Sides	Walnut	⅜"	¾"	4½" (a)
	1	Bottom	Walnut	⅜"	¾"	4⅜"

NOTES:

(a) Dimension listed is working size; part will be shortened when shaped.

(b) Identical in construction to larger holder, but Front and Back are listed separately here because they are different thickness.w

Vintage Recipe Box

I FIGURED THAT NO BOOK OF kitchen projects is complete without something to hold recipes. But in this age of smart phones and iPads (like the one I used to display a recipe in the earlier Knife Block Tablet Holder project), I thought that any recipe box I planned to include here had to be somewhat out of the ordinary.

But that was the problem: Recipe boxes, by their nature, are pretty ordinary and old-fashioned to begin with these days. That's when it occurred to me to make one that was literally old-fashioned, based on the vintage boxes of yesteryear.

The design of this box was pretty common in the early 20th century. So common, in fact, that thousands were made and sold by kitchen suppliers along with – and as advertisement for – their other products. For several decades the Washburn-Crosby Co., the original makers of Gold Medal Flour, sold small wooden boxes with a full set of recipe cards for about a dollar. The style, hardware and size of the boxes varied only slightly over the years, but all were made of oak with box-jointed corners and every one of them, of course, had an ad for Gold Medal Flour pasted inside the lid.

The box presented here is patterned on original boxes from around 1930, but I did change the size of the box joints. Originals typically had ³⁄₁₆" joints, but I bumped those up to ¼" to make it easier to work with. If you want to customize the box to a different size – the math is a breeze.

Recipe boxes either had small leaf hinges attached to the back or the pivoting hinge I've re-created for this project. If you don't want to make your own pivot hinges, it's fine to use any small pair of leaf hinges on the back – it'll still be authentic to the period.

BOXING THE JOINT

Begin by cutting your ¼" stock to size for all six components. Although my hand is partially blocking it in **PHOTO 1**, I've set the stop on my

Cut stock to size. A miter-gauge stop – partially hidden by my hand – ensures identical workpieces.

To keep everything straight when cutting box joints, clear labeling of the parts is a necessity.

Set the distance from the bit to the guide rail. Setup bars like these in common sizes are great shop accessories.

miter gauge to ensure that the ends, sides and the top/bottom are all in matched pairs.

Balance the box sides and ends for the box sides and ends on a flat surface, and let the box fall open. Arranged as in **PHOTO 2**, mark the sides clearly in pencil. To help keep everything in the correct orientation when cutting the joints, mark the top edge of all four pieces, the sides with A and the ends with B. Since you'll be flipping these pieces over when cutting, it's helpful to mark both sides.

For large projects I almost always use a box-joint jig on the table saw, but for smaller boxes like this you can't beat the router-table jig you'll see here. While jigs like this vary, they all use an index mechanism – usually a pin or rail – sized

to match the width of the fingers of the joint, which helps ensure consistent spacing.

Set the jig so the guide rail is ¼" from the router bit and lock down the jig. In **PHOTO 3** I'm using a brass setup bar, which I know exactly matches the bit diameter. (Tip: You can also use the shank of a ¼" drill bit.)

Now, set the bit height, which controls how deep the box joints are. This time, instead of using a setup bar I'm using one of the workpieces themselves, since the joint depth must exactly match the stock thickness. (**PHOTO 4**)

Starting with an end B piece, make the first cut by holding the workpiece against the jig's sliding fence, and the top edge against the

Set the bit height by using one of the work-pieces.

With the first workpiece up against the guide rail, make the initial cut.

Move the first joint over the guide rail and make the rest of the cuts in the first workpiece.

Using the previous workpieces as a spacer, make the first cut in the second workpiece.

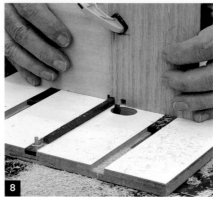

As before, just keep moving the piece over to the guide rail to make the rest of the cuts.

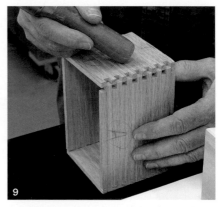

Test fit the joints. If they're a bit tight, tap the assembly lightly into place.

guide rail, as in **PHOTO 5**. Note that I'm also using a small clamp to help secure the small workpiece as I push it through the spinning bit.

With the jig's fence back at the starting position, reposition the workpiece so the first cut rides the guide rail, and run it over the bit again, as in **PHOTO 6**. Continue this process along the entire edge of the workpiece till all the joints are cut.

Now, use this B workpiece as a guide for the mating A workpiece by reversing it so the opposite face is against the fence, and the top edge is still oriented toward the guide rail. With the top finger over the rail, it acts as a spacer that keeps the top edge of the A workpiece correctly located as you make the first cut. (**PHOTO 7**) With the first cut complete, set the B piece aside and continue cutting the A piece as you

did before by moving it over one notch after every cut. (**PHOTO 8**) Repeat for each remaining workpiece in turn, then flip all four over and run through the process again in the same order to cut the joints on the opposite edges.

With all the fingers cut, dry-assemble the box to check for fit. The joints will probably be a bit snug, so you may need to lightly tap the pieces together for the assembly as I'm doing with the wooden end of a small mallet in **PHOTO 9**.

If you're satisfied with the fit, sand and remove any markings from the inner surfaces (easier now than after assembly), apply glue to the joints and clamp it. In **PHOTO 10**, I'm using some ¼" box joint clamping cauls that put exact pressure on every one of the joint fingers. This keeps things square while the glue dries. By the

way, go sparingly on the glue! It doesn't take much for a secure joint – which is already plenty strong to begin with. Use too much and you'll have to clean up a lot of squeeze-out.

Complete the box assembly by gluing and clamping the bottom and top into place. (**PHOTO 11**) This is just a plain butt joint attachment, but the box is so small that wood movement simply isn't an issue here.

PUT A LID ON IT

When the glue-up has dried, give the entire box a good sanding to smooth out the joinery seams, then transfer the cut line for the box lid from the Recipe Box End View drawing on page 45. Notice that the cut line is placed so it goes right on top of a lengthwise finger on the front, and curves through a lengthwise finger in back, confining the cuts to solid

10

Box joint cauls and a band clamp make fast work of the glue-up, and keep everything square.

11

Glue and clamp the box bottom and top into place.

12

Cut the lid free of the completed box on the band saw.

13

Escutcheon pins hold the hinges in place.

wood – no joint is bridged by the cut.

Remove the lid on the band saw, following the cut line exactly and as smoothly as possible. In **PHOTO 12**, I've swapped my everyday ½" blade for a fine-cut ¼" blade to make the cut. The idea here is you want the curved cut to be as smooth and accurate as possible to minimize sanding those edges afterward.

The box is complete and ready for whatever finish you prefer. Back in the 1930s the finish would have been shellac so feel free to use that, but I opted for a satin polyurethane for the highest protection.

These boxes had either regular leaf hinges installed on the back, or pivot hinges on the sides. It's easiest to go with leaf hinges, but I wanted to include an example of the pivot hinge. This is simply a thin piece of metal – it would have been brass

or light steel – about ¼" wide. I cut mine to 1⁷⁄₁₆" from a piece of ¼" brass stock you can find at any home center or hardware store using a rotary tool with a cutoff wheel, then rounded the ends with a disc sander. I've included a close-up of the hinge and mounting points in the Hinge Detail drawing on page 45. Note how the mounting pins go into the centers of the box-joint fingers.

With the box taped closed, lay out and mark the box for the hinges, taking care that the holes are in the centers of the fingers. Drill pilot holes – I clipped the head off an escutcheon pin and used that for piloting – then tap in the escutcheon pins, as in **PHOTO 13**. The lid end of the hinge receives two pins, while a single pin goes into the body of the box.

I added one last touch to my recipe box, and that was to look around

online to find an old Gold Medal label of the type used in the boxes back in the 1930s. I printed it out and attached it to the inside of the lid just like on the originals, capping off the authentic appearance of this classic home for my favorite recipes.

These boxes varied slightly in dimensions, but almost all were sized to use 3x5 cards, the most common cards in use back in the day. Of course, you can enlarge the box to accommodate 4x6 or any other size recipe cards you prefer. Likewise, feel free to stain the box for a darker appearance and a better match to your kitchen decor.

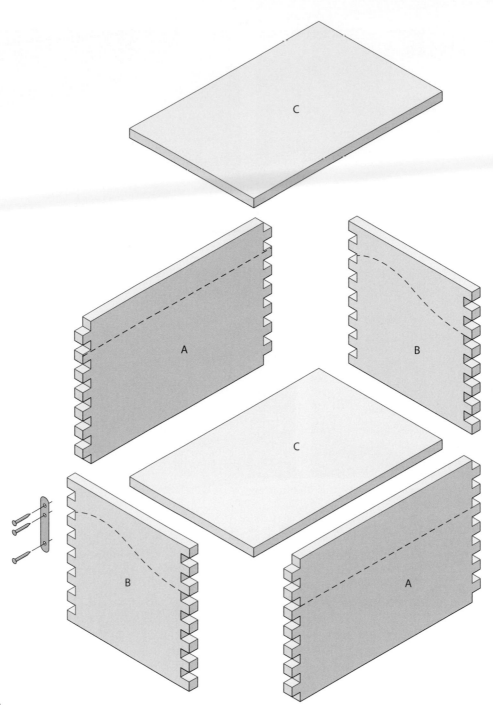

EXPLODED VIEW

VINTAGE RECIPE BOX CUT LIST

Overall Dimensions: 5¾" long x 3¾" deep x 4¼" tall

REF	QTY	PART	STOCK	THICKNESS	WIDTH	LENGTH
A	2	Front/Back	Oak	¼"	3¾"	5¾"
B	2	Ends	Oak	¼"	3¾"	3¾"
C	2	Top/Bottom	Oak	¼"	3¾"	5¾"

ADDITIONAL MATERIALS:

Shop-made Hinges, ¼" x 1⁷⁄₁₆" made from .064"-thick brass stock, or other small hinges (2 needed)

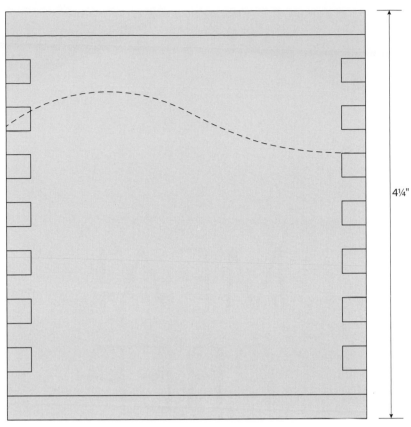

END VIEW

4¼"

3¾"

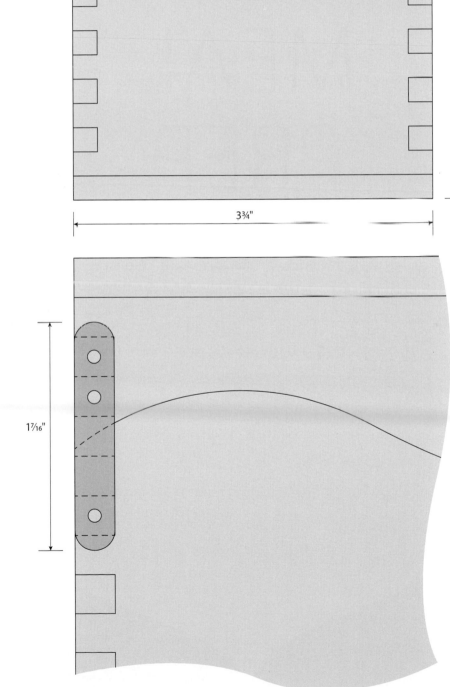

1⁷⁄₁₆"

HINGE DETAIL

MEAL
PREP

✦

WHEN I'M OUT IN MY WORKSHOP, TIME AND TROUBLES

seem to disappear. It's the same thing in my other workshop – the kitchen.

✦ And just like when working with wood, preparing a great meal has

similar processes and tools. Woodworkers know that a satisfying project

results from a combination of talent, technique and tools – and it's no

different in the kitchen. And just as preparing a workpiece in the shop

requires the appropriate tools, you'd demand no less while cooking. ✦

So as you start working on that next glorious dinner, any one of the

projects that follow will help you get the job done right.

✦

Sink Board

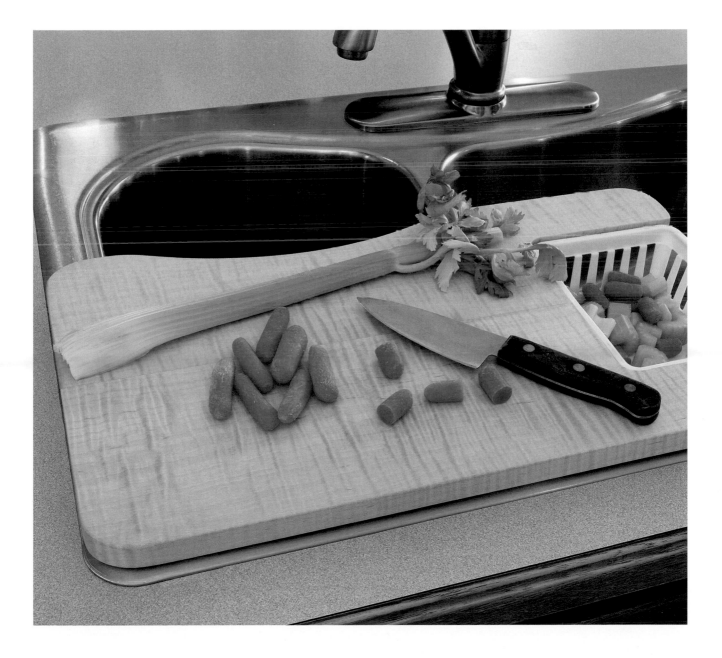

AS WITH THE RECIPE BOX IN the previous chapter, I figured a cutting board was a must for a book of kitchen projects. In fact, we'll have a couple variations on culinary boards, but none will be just "plain ol' boards." This project, designed to fit a divided sink and with a drainage basket to collect freshly cut food, is a good example.

Like many projects in this book, this sink board is fitted to existing kitchen dimensions as well as to the properties of the drainage basket I used. However, it's a simple matter to match this to your own sink and basket with just a few dimensional changes.

This project marks the first appearance here of some really nice-looking figured maple I found a while back. You'll see it again in a couple other projects, but you can really use any closed-grain hardwood you'd like. Maple, cherry and walnut are all good choices, as is teak, although it can be tough to work with. Don't use oak, as it's filled with nooks and crannies that bacteria would love to call home.

MEASURE TWICE
I've already talked a lot about measuring in earlier chapters, but this sink board design fits a sink exactly, so the measurements are a bit more critical. With that in mind, your first task is to head into your kitchen with a tape measure or rule. (**PHOTO 1**) The key measurement for a divided sink is the exact space between the inner surface on one side and the inner surface of the center divider. We'll install some cleats on the underside that hold it in place when in use, so measure carefully. By the way, for a divided sink you can plan your board for either side, but I recommend making it for the side where the garbage disposal is located, if you have one.

Now there's a second measuring task. What makes this cutting board so handy is that it has a recessed basket you can move the cut food to. The basket has drainage, so once

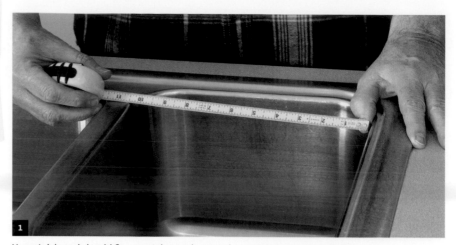

1

Your sink board should fit your sink exactly, so make sure to measure carefully.

2

Find a basket styled and sized the way you like, then design your sink board around it.

3

For a good, watertight joint, running both halves of the sink board over a jointer is a must.

filled with freshly cut veggies you can easily rinse it right in the basket. In **PHOTO 2**, you can see several good candidates. You can use almost any kind of small basket or colander, even a metal strainer if you cut off the wire handle. The only real requirement is that the basket have a lip of some kind that allows it to rest in an opening in the board. For this project, I picked one of those square baskets in the back left of this photo. I got a package of three of them at Walmart for about a dollar.

Get two key measurements from the basket. The first is the overall width and length, measured right at the basket's top edge. The second is the width and length minus that lip around the top. These two measurements will help us cut the opening

and size a rabbet to fit the basket perfectly. More on this later.

BUILD A BOARD
It's always best to make a cutting board out of two or more narrower pieces. Cutting boards made from a single piece of wood are prone to warping, but laminating narrower pieces helps minimize this since the growth rings don't extend across the width of the board. If possible, alternate the growth rings.

Cut the stock to size and prepare the mating edges. You want a really tight joint here, so a trip across a jointer – or treatment with a handplane – is essential for a good glue joint. (**PHOTO 3**)

Water-resistant or waterproof glue is also a must for cutting boards, since

Apply glue to the mating edges of the board and clamp up till dry

Give the glue squeeze-out a few minutes to stiffen, then scrape it off.

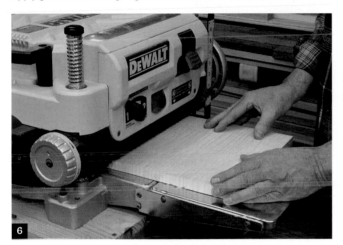

Dress the board surface with a quick trip through the planer.

Mark the board for cutting curves, openings and the overall shape.

they're exposed to a lot of moisture with use and washing. Apply glue to the mating edges of your stock, and then clamp the workpiece up securely. (**PHOTO 4**)

You'll get some squeeze-out, of course, which you can wipe off immediately with a damp rag. I find that wiping tends to spread it around a lot more than I'd like, so I prefer to let the glue set up a bit until it turns kind of rubbery, then scrape it off, as in **PHOTO 5**. Removal is much cleaner this way.

When the glue has fully cured, level the board surface with a scraper, plane or by sanding, or give it a quick run through a planer. (**PHOTO 6**) However you level the surface, take as little material off as possible. We're not thicknessing the board here, just dressing it.

Now, lay out the board for cutting by transferring the Sink Board Pattern from page 52 to the best-looking side. Since you'll be custom-sizing and shaping your board to match your sink, the pattern included here can act as a guide, but tweak it as needed. (**PHOTO 7**)

First, transfer the smaller of the two basket measurements to one end of the board. This is the measurement taken at the base of the lip and establishes the opening. Now, mark the four corners of the board for rounding-off to match the round corners of your sink. In my case, tracing a small measuring cup was the perfect size. Tracing around a small plastic container I use for holding tacks worked well for rounding the

corners of the basket opening. Finally, I created a curve at the front of the board, as in **PHOTO 7**. This provides an opening at the top of the board to scrape peelings and cuttings into the sink for a one-way trip through the garbage disposal. This opening at the front also allows me to run water in front of the board while working.

BASKET CASE

Cut the opening for the basket on the end of the board. You can do this with a jigsaw, as in **PHOTO 8**, on the band saw, or with a handsaw. For the cleanest cut possible, dial down the rotary action on the jigsaw as low as it will go and use a fine-cut blade rated for hardwood. Also at this time round off the four outside corners. We'll do the two corners at the bas-

Cut out the basket opening on the end of the board.

Rout a ¼" x ¼" rabbet around the upper edge of the basket opening to create a ledge.

ket opening after the next step.

Create a ledge on the opening for the basket to rest in with a router fitted with a rabbeting bit sized to match the lip of the basket. (**PHOTO 9**) The rabbet should be wide enough that the basket nestles in easily, and deep enough that the top edge of the basket is below the board surface. A ¼" x ¼" rabbet worked perfectly for me, but size yours accordingly. Once you've created the rabbet, go ahead and round off those two corners on the end of the opening.

Grab your board and a short pencil and head back into the kitchen, then set the board on the sink so it fits evenly over the sink rim at the side and front. Hold the board firmly in place, then reach under the board and trace the sink opening onto the underside. You'll end up with a U shape on the board that defines the edges of the sink opening.

Cut your cleats and line them up on the inside edges of your marking, then countersink and temporarily attach them to the underside of the board with exterior-grade or other water-resistant screws, as in **PHOTO 10**. One long cleat goes on each side, and the short one on the front.

Remove the cleats and give the entire board a good sanding. I normally find that sanding up to #150-grit is good for most projects, but

for a cutting board you want the smoothest surface possible so sand through #220-grit or even a little higher. (**PHOTO 11**)

Reattach the cleats, and the board is complete and ready for the finish of your choice. As discussed in the opening chapter, all commercial finishes are food-safe. I used several coats of thinned Danish oil – an oil/varnish blend – that soaked deeply into the wood. As each coat cured I followed with a quick, light rubbing with #400-grit sandpaper. The idea here is that I wanted the finish in the wood, not on the surface where it might abrade off with knife use.

The last step depends on your basket. If it already has drainage you're ready to head into the kitchen and start chopping. If not, create drainage by marking out a grid on the bottom of the basket and simply drilling a series of holes, as in **PHOTO 12**. Holes of ³⁄₁₆" to ¼" will work well.

Finally, depending on the design of your sink you may need to do one more thing. In some sinks the divider is at the same level as the rim around the sink. If that's the case you need do nothing more. However, on most sinks – link mine – the divider is recessed just a bit. If it is, you'll find that the sink board will tend to wobble. It's supported all the way around the left and bottom ends, but

not over that divider.

This is easily fixable by just adding a small shim next to the cleat on that side to make up the difference in the level of the recessed divider. This little shim can be simply glued into place, as in **PHOTO 13**.

Customize your sink board any way you like. The basket you use will dictate much of your customization, of course, but you can also rearrange its location. I like to scrape waste off the front into the sink and move the chopped veggies into the basket at the right, but you can reorder this. Or, put the basket on the left instead. The key is to make it in the most efficient manner for the way you work.

One note on the baskets: Plastic baskets are usually designed to stack, and so most have small tabs under the lip at the top that prevent them getting stuck. (If you look closely at **PHOTO 2**, you can see these on the white baskets.) You'll need to cut these off to allow the basket to nestle down into its opening in the board.

10

Attach the holding cleats to the underside of the board with exterior-grade screws.

11

Give everything a thorough sanding up to at least #220-grit.

12

Drill a series of holes in the bottom of your basket if it doesn't already have drainage.

13

If your sink has a recessed center divider, you'll need to add a small shim to steady the board.

SINK BOARD CUT LIST

Overall Dimensions: 1¾" x 11" x 19" (including cleats)

REF	QTY	PART	STOCK	THICKNESS	WIDTH	LENGTH
A	1	Main Board	Maple	¾"	11"	19"
B	2	Cleats	Maple	¾"	1"	6"
C	1	Short Cleat	Maple	¾"	1"	2"

ADDITIONAL MATERIALS:

Plastic or Metal Mesh Basket

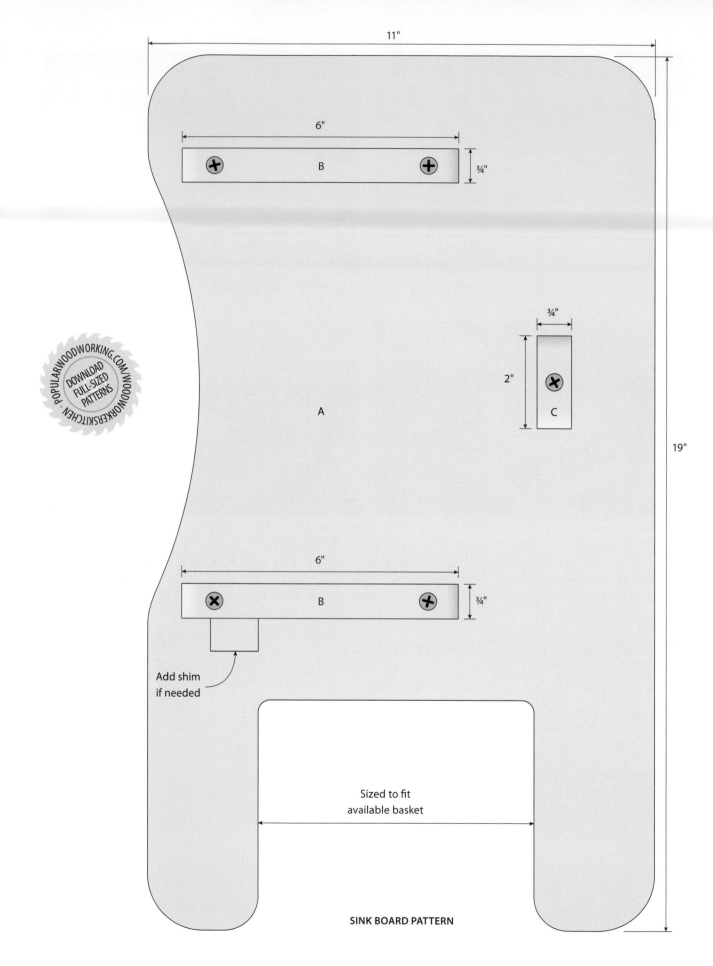

11"

6"

B

¾"

¾"

2"

C

A

19"

6"

B

¾"

Add shim
if needed

Sized to fit
available basket

SINK BOARD PATTERN

DOWNLOAD
FULL-SIZED
PATTERNS

POPULARWOODWORKING.COM/WOODWORKERSKITCHEN

Rolling Pin

ROLLING PINS ARE EASY TO FIND
and purchase, but it's both easy and
more satisfying to make your own.
I'd originally planned to make this a
lathe project (and, of course, you can
turn your own rolling pin on a lathe
if you'd like – I have), but instead decided to make this one of the easiest
projects in the book. You can make a
pin like this in just an hour or two,
and make it exactly the size you want.

What makes this project especially easy is that there are only two
components – a roller body and a pair
of handles – and you can find them
almost ready to go from just about
any woodworking supplier and even
many home centers. The roller body
is a baseball bat turning blank, often
called a billet, while the handles are
large Shaker pegs.

Commercially available rolling pin
diameters are all over the board,
with non-handled rod or French pins
generally less than 2". Handled pins,
meanwhile, typically range from 2½"
to 3", although I've seen some smaller
and a few 4" whoppers. The baseball
bat billet used here is 2¾", so it's
about mid-range as far as typical
diameters go.

I selected a maple billet, a common
species used for pins, but any heavy
closed-grain wood is fine. There's
food contact here, so an open-grained
wood like ash (common for baseball
bats) or oak is a definite no-no.

GETTING STARTED

Examine your billet and check for
knots or cracks and measure out a
portion sized to the pin you want
that avoids these potential issues,
then simply cut the roller body to
length. I cut this one to 12" on the
band saw, but note in **PHOTO 1** that
I've clamped it to my miter gauge.
Round objects can be difficult to cut
with power equipment unless firmly
secured or held in some type of jig
that keeps them from spinning. If
you have any doubts, clamp the billet
to a workbench or in a vise, and cut
it by hand.

Clean up the cut ends to remove

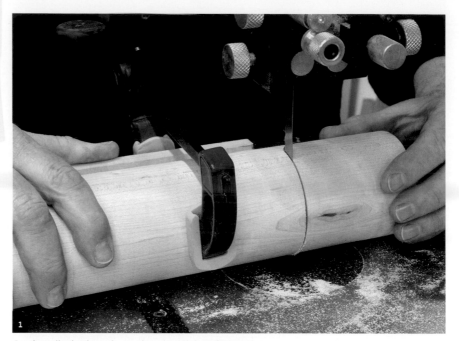

Cut the roller body to the working length best for you.

saw marks. (**PHOTO 2**) Start with
coarse paper and work up through
finer grits. For anything that actually comes into contact with food,
especially raw food, I like to sand to
#220-grit or higher for the smoothest
surface possible.

Mark the ends of the roller on-
center. The center finder in **PHOTO
3** comes in handy all the time in my
shop, and if you don't have one I
highly recommend them.

Drill vertical holes on your marks
sized to accept the tenons on the
Shaker peg handles. Large pegs
like these usually have ¾" tenons,
but measure to be sure. These holes
should be as straight as possible so
the handles are neatly aligned when
glued into place, so a drill press is the
tool of choice here. (**PHOTO 4**)

Test fit the peg tenons and adjust
with sandpaper as needed (they may
be slightly tapered), then apply glue
to the drilled holes on the roller body
and a bit on the shoulder under the
peg. Insert the pegs, remove any glue
squeeze-out and clamp up till dry.
(**PHOTO 5**) I found it easier to glue
and clamp the handles one at a time.

Give the roller body a thorough

sanding along its length. These billets
are pretty rough on the outside from
the manufacturing process – they're
intended for lathe turning and so
no real care is taken for a smooth
surface – but you'll want the roller as
smooth as possible. In **PHOTO 6** I'm
starting with a coarse #80-grit paper
to remove the ring-like scoring left
by the manufacturer. A sanding block
helps to do the leveling. Once the billet was generally smooth I sanded by
hand up through #220-grit. This is a
food surface, remember, so you want
nothing for pastry to lodge in.

Your rolling pin can be left raw
– many commercial ones are – but
a light oil finish that cures in the
wood keeps the surface smooth and
helps discourage water from soaking
in when washed. Any finish you'd
use on a cutting board will work fine
here. As with the Sink Board project in the previous chapter, I used a
thinned oil/varnish blend and sanded
the surface with #400-grit paper after
it was cured for a silky smooth pin.

Sand the saw marks from the cut ends of the roller body.

Mark the centers of the roller body ends for drilling.

Drill holes in the roller body ends sized to accept the handle tenons.

Sand the saw marks from the cut ends of the roller body.

Give the roller body a thorough sanding up to at least #220-grit.

ROLLING PIN CUT LIST

Overall Dimensions: 2¾" x 21"

QTY	PART	STOCK	THICK	WIDTH	LENGTH
1	Roller Body	Maple Billet	2¾"	n/a	12" (a)
2	Handles	Maple	¾"	n/a	4½" (b)

NOTES:

(a) Roller body is made from a maple billet, often sold as turning blanks for baseball bats. A billet of any closed-grain wood species may be used.

(b) Handles are Shaker pegs measuring 4½" in length, not including tenon. Thickness listed is tenon diameter.

Veggie or Pastry Scraper

CUTTING VEGETABLES INTO little pieces makes for a lot of, well, little pieces. You can always just dump them into your cooking vessel right from a cutting board. But if the board's large – or if the pieces are widely scattered as they sometimes are after dicing – getting them transferred can lead to a lot of strays on the stove or floor. And the "dumping them off the cutting board" part isn't even an option if prepping directly on a countertop, as you might for working pastry.

For those times, a scraper is invaluable. The thin wooden edge won't hurt countertops, and the general shape helps a scraper act as a third hand, easily corralling and scooping things up. For pastry, the thin edge readily lifts anything stuck to the prep surface.

Scrapers can be any size or shape as long as one edge is thin, and the other easy to grasp. In this project we'll make three different versions of basically the same scraper and you can decide which you like best – or design one of your own.

Since you'll be working with raw food, closed-grained wood is best for scrapers. I had a quantity of nicely figured maple left over from the Sink Board project and opted for that, but any hardwood is fine as long as it's not open-grained. The scrapers shown here measure 4¾" square, but make yours any size you like.

ONE CUT, TWO SCRAPERS

Resawing thick stock on the band saw is always a good way to conserve wood – especially figured maple – without sending it to the dust collector as chips when using the planer. However, with some careful cutting it also creates duplicate workpieces. Since these scrapers are essentially wedges, by resawing at an angle, you'll end up with two identical scraper blanks.

Set up your band saw table at an appropriate angle, which will vary depending on the workpiece size. For the scrapers here the angle was

1 With the table tilted, resaw the workpiece into two matching sections.

2 Trim off the back edge if desired for symmetry.

3 Slightly round over the handle end, then work through the grits for a smooth sanding all around.

about 7½°, but to be honest I know that only because I looked after setting the table. I found it easier, and you probably will too, to set the angle so the blade goes through opposite corners of the workpiece when cutting. You can see what I mean in **PHOTO 1**. Also in this photo you can see how I'm keeping my fingers away by using a push block I made just for resawing. It's just two pieces of scrap of the same thickness as my workpiece overlapped and glued together. (Don't use nails or screws in case you cut into the push block at the completion of the cut.)

You'll notice here that I've made the cut so that the grain will run side-to-side in the finished scraper, but you can do yours in either direction. The reason I've chosen the crosswise

grain orientation is that if the scraper ever warps – and it will – the leading edge always remains flat to your work surface.

I used a workpiece ⅞" thick; following the cut and later sanding, that gives me a scraper with the handle end about ¾" thick. If you'd like a heftier handle, just use a thicker workpiece and adjust the table tilt.

Since these wedges are right angles at the handle end, I also flipped each over while my band saw table was still tilted and shaved off a slight bit of stock on the high end of that right angle, as in **PHOTO 2**. This makes the handle end symmetrical and, at least for me, easier to work.

Next, round off the sharp edges on the handle end with a sanding block. (**PHOTO 3**) When finished, the

For version one, center a hole in the handle with a 1¼" Forstner bit.

Make the finger grooves for version two on the router table.

Taper the sides and cut the rounded end of version three on the band saw, then sand the handle with a disc sander.

handles were rounded nicely. At the same time, take some of the sharpness off the scraper end – a resulting edge of about ¹⁄₁₆" is good. When done, give the scraper a good general sanding with increasingly finer grits.

By the way, for version three of the scraper – which has a curved handle – no need to sand the handle end yet.

Essentially, the scraper is now done and you could head straight to the kitchen, but I thought it would be nice to present three different design elements. All three are reflected in the Scraper Patterns on page 59.

MAKE IT YOUR WAY

For the first one, I drilled a 1¼" hole about 1" on-center from the edge of

the handle. A Forstner bit works well for this. You can see in **PHOTO 4** that I'm angling the bit slightly as I drill to match the wedge angle.

In version two, a continuous finger groove runs across both sides of the scraper handle. For this, a ¾" round bit in the router table works great. These bits go by a couple names such as bullnose, fluting and core box bits, but they all cut a round-bottomed groove in the workpiece. Set the table fence so the center of the groove is about ¾" from the handle end (the groove edge will be about ⅜" from the end of the handle). Run it through on one side, then flip it over and run it again on the other side. Note in **PHOTO 5** that I'm using

a piece of scrap as a push block for both safety and ease of handling the cut.

For version three, I taped a scrap wedge to serve as a spacer so the scraper blank would be a square workpiece, then cut the profile from the Scraper Patterns on the band saw. A disc sander smooths the curved handle end. (**PHOTO 6**)

All that's left now is to give your scrapers a final sanding – as with most of the food-contact projects here, I went up to #400-grit for an extra smooth surface – followed by the finish of your choice.

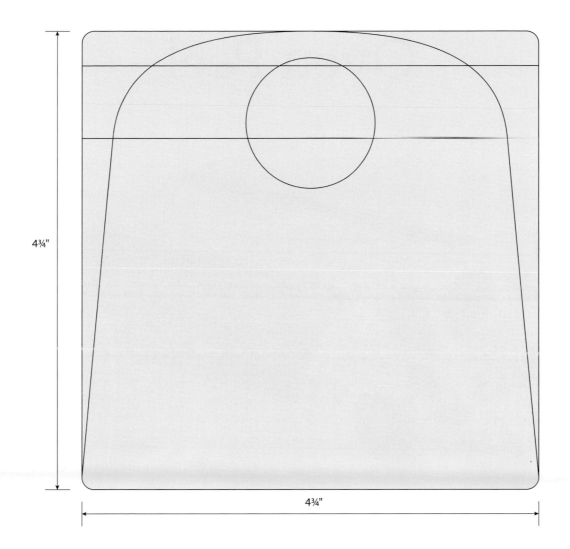

4¾"

4¾"

SCRAPER PATTERNS

SCRAPER CUT LIST
Overall Dimensions: 4¾" x 4¾" x ¾"

QTY	PART	STOCK	THICKNESS	WIDTH	LENGTH
1	Main Workpiece	Maple	⅞"	4¾"	4¾"

NOTES:
Any closed-grain hardwood may be used

Oven Peel

AS YOU'VE PROBABLY NOTICED by now, nearly every project in this book is customizable, either to tweak them to your personal tastes or needs, or to better match hardware, glassware and other supplies that might be different from what I used. None of the projects, however, are as customizable as this one – or as versatile.

You can use this as a pizza peel, bread peel or sandwich peel, which is why I've opted to call this simply an oven peel. It also makes a great cutting board for general kitchen use. On the dining table, its length makes it perfect for serving and cutting French, Italian or other long loaves of bread. After dinner, it's a handy tray for toting dishes and such back to the kitchen.

It can also be made of any hardwood you like (it's another great project for putting random scraps to use), and although mine uses seven pieces you can make it with any number and arrangement of workpieces when doing the glue-up.

Most importantly, make it any size you want. If your specialty is nice, big pizzas, make it wider and shorter. For just bread, it can be narrower and shorter. If you have a large oven or plan to use it with the grill, lengthen the handle.

My wife, Sally, and I love personal pizzas made from 8" Boboli pizza shells – they're a movie-night staple in our house – so the 9" x 17" open portion is perfect for two pizzas. And when I'm batching it anytime Sally's out of town, nothing goes with a cold beer and a sci-fi movie like a toasted sandwich prepped on this long peel and slid into the oven.

When doing your customization, stick with closed-grain woods – food can lodge in open-grained species like oak. Also, because this peel is thin, it's best to laminate the board workpieces with the grain alternated; a thin peel like this will tend to warp if made from any single workpiece that's not rift- or quartersawn.

For the strongest glue-up possible, thoroughly joint the mating edges of each workpiece.

Arranging the workpieces so the growth rings alternate helps minimize warping over time.

Glue and clamp the workpieces together, alternating the clamps top-to-bottom for a flat glue-up.

Plane the workpiece to a uniform thickness; ⅜" to ½" is good.

LAMINATE THE WORKPIECE

Get started by cutting your stock to size as needed to match the desired width and length of your finished peel. Since this will be a laminated board that'll take a lot of abuse, joint the mating edges of each piece to give the best gluing surface possible. (**PHOTO 1**)

With everything cut and prepped, do some test arrangements on your workbench or table. Check the end grain, as in **PHOTO 2**, alternating growth rings across the width to help keep the finished peel flat.

Spread water-resistant or waterproof glue on the mating surfaces of each workpiece and clamp up. (**PHOTO 3**) Once clamped, be sure to remove glue squeeze-out before it completely dries. Note how I've alternated the clamps top-to-bottom to distribute clamping pressure. Not doing so might end up in a curved board when you take it out of the clamps.

When the workpiece has cured, remove the clamps and scrape off any dried glue, then plane to the desired thickness. (**PHOTO 4**) Oven peels vary in thickness, and if you plan to use it only as a peel you can opt for ⅜" for a nice, light board. However, this one will see use in my kitchen as both a peel and a cutting board, so I've planed to ½".

Transfer the Peel Pattern from page 63 to the workpiece, or create your own. To draw the curved front, make a basic trammel by drilling a pencil hole in one end of some long scrap and driving a nail at the other end at the desired curve radius. In **PHOTO 5**, I've selected a curve radius of 13½". Hang on to this trammel; we'll use it again later.

SHAPING THE PEEL

Now, cut out your peel. In **PHOTO 6**, I'm using a band saw, but a jigsaw or scrollsaw will also handle the task. Follow this by sanding all the

My quick-and-dirty trammel easily draws the curve for the front of the peel.

Cut out the overall shape on the band saw or with a jigsaw.

Sand and refine the cut edge as needed with a disc sander and, seen here, a spindle sander.

With the appropriate bit in your router table, round over all edges except the front.

Clamp the workpiece to a solid work surface, and use a rasp or other tool to bevel the front edge.

Spread out some newspaper to catch any splatters or splashes, and give your oven peel the finish of your choice.

cuts you've just made. (**PHOTO 7**) A combination of a disc sander for the convex curves and spindle sander for concave curves makes quick work of removing saw marks, but by hand with a sanding block works just fine.

You can skip this next step if you'd like, but I think a rounded edge not only makes boards like this more attractive, but also easier to handle. You can do this with a random orbit sander or even with some aggressive sanding with a sanding block, but this is where a router outfitted with a roundover bit really shines. In **PHOTO 8**, I used the router table extension of my table saw, but use a handheld router if you prefer.

To make it easier to slide food onto and off of the peel, let's bevel the front edge to a nice taper. For the shallow taper on the project peel, pencil in a parallel guideline 1½" back from the front edge. Grab your trammel and place the pivot point 1½" farther back on the peel surface

than you did earlier, and draw the curve on the front. Now, use a rasp or forming tool to remove stock in a straight taper between this guideline and the front edge, as in **PHOTO 9**. If you have a reciprocating saw or grinder, you can speed this process up by first removing most of the waste and then refining the taper with the forming tool.

When you're satisfied with the taper, remove tool marks (you'll have plenty) with sandpaper wrapped around a wood block to keep the surface level as you sand. Start with coarse paper and work up to finer grits till all the marks are gone and the taper is smooth. Follow this by giving the entire peel a good sanding. I sanded up to #220-grit, but feel free to go a bit higher for an even smoother surface.

By the way, peels can be beveled on just the top as I've chosen here, or on both top and bottom. If you decide on the latter, make the bevel on the

underside very short, maybe between ¼" and ⅜" – you just don't need that much of a taper underneath.

At this point you can consider your peel done if you like; for many peels, especially those used simply for getting things in and out of the oven, the wood is left raw. Since this one will have multiple uses in my kitchen and dining room, however, I wanted it to look as nice as possible.

As you can see in **PHOTO 10**, several coats of oil finish really bring out the color of the cherry and the beautiful figure of the tiger maple I used.

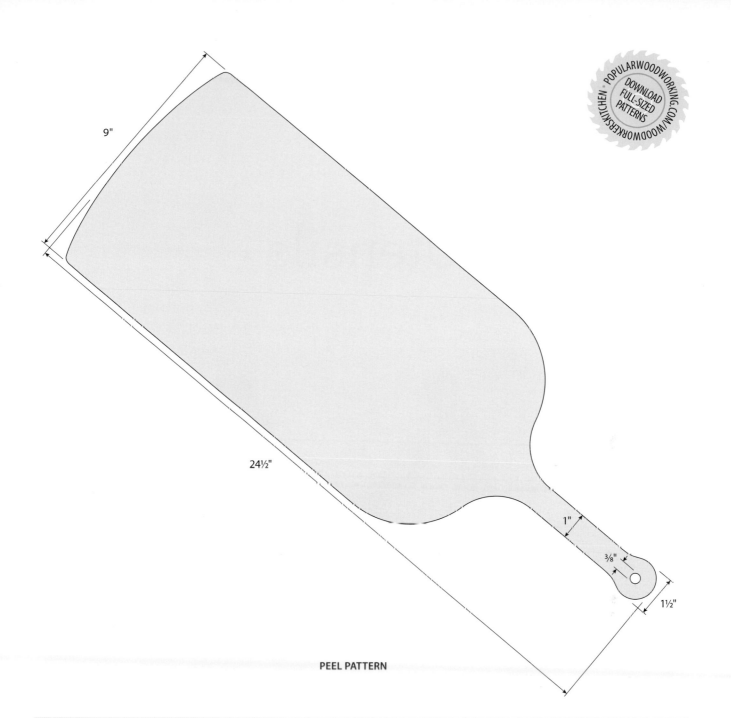

PEEL PATTERN

9"

24½"

1"

³⁄₈"

1½"

OVEN PEEL CUT LIST

Overall Dimensions: ½" x 9" x 24½"

QTY	PART	STOCK	THICKNESS	WIDTH	LENGTH
1	Handle Workpiece	Cherry	¾"	2½"	25"
4	Body Workpieces	Maple	¾"	1½"	19"
2	Trim Workpieces	Cherry	¾"	¼"	19"

NOTES:

Rough stock of the dimensions shown above was used to create the blank, which was then planed to ½" thick and cut to final dimensions after glue-up.

Any closed-grained hardwood may be used.

Although the project peel is made with seven workpieces, any number and width of components may be used to create a final project of any desired width.

11

Utensils

HARDWOOD UTENSILS, OFTEN called treenware, are a staple of high-end craft markets and upscale kitchen shops. They feel great in the hand and are wonderful to use in the kitchen.

They're so smooth and intricately shaped, it stands to reason that they must be really hard to make. No wonder utensils like this are on the expensive side.

Guess what? As elegant as these are, they're not difficult to create at all. In fact, not only are they fairly easy to do, but they lend themselves to be made in multiples limited only by the size of the original main workpiece. With some careful planning and a bit of creativity with shaping and design, you could easily get a dozen or two utensils out of single block of wood.

Cherry is probably the most popular wood used for these, followed by walnut and maple, but any closed-grain hardwood is fine. This is a food-contact item, so open-grained woods aren't suitable.

As an aside, the block of cherry you'll see in this chapter came from a downed tree at my parents' home in Pennsylvania two decades ago. My dad and I cut and stacked a bunch of it and I've used that cherry for countless projects over the years. This piece is the last one I had squirreled away in my shop, and since my mom was an avid cook (where do you think I learned?), it seemed fitting to use the last piece in my inventory for a cooking-related project.

BEGINNING THOUGHTS

You can use any big chunk of wood to make utensils, but you'll find it easier, more efficient and even safer if that chunk is square or rectangular in cross section. Laying out the patterns on the wood is straightforward, cutting is more precise, a square workpiece maximizes the number of items you can cut from it, and always having at least one square, flat surface on the saw table makes it far easier to handle when cutting. With that

Cut out the first utensil on the band saw, using the marked pattern as a guide.

Before starting the second utensil, I found it handy to go ahead and do a quick sanding of the workpiece's cut face.

Cut the second utensil as the first, then repeat to create as many as the workpiece will provide.

in mind, if your main workpiece isn't square, head over to the jointer or planer and make it so.

You can mark several patterns on your workpiece before starting, but I find it easier to do them one at a time. Cutting curves and shapes for utensils is a very freeform experience done almost more by touch than following exact lines, and you'll likely find that you tend to not follow the lines that closely. Which, of course, would affect any other patterns already drawn onto the wood.

In the photos that follow, I'll illustrate the process for creating two large spatulas for outdoor grilling. Since the process is the same no matter what you're cutting I won't include specific instructions for them, but I'll also make a smaller spatula

for the kitchen as well as a couple more items I'll describe later.

Start by drawing the first pattern on the wood along one edge. Now, head over to the band saw and cut the pattern out, as in **PHOTO 1**. Two passes through the blade is all it takes for this first step.

Mark the second spatula below where the first utensil was just cut out. The side profile of this second will be slightly different, since the bottom edge of the first one now becomes the top edge of the second. It goes without saying that when making these they're kind of like snowflakes: no two from a single workpiece will look quite the same.

Before cutting the second out, I like to give the cut face a quick rudimentary sanding, as in **PHOTO 2**.

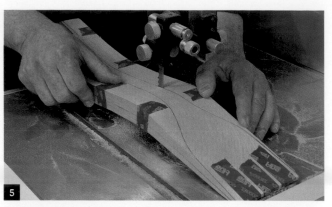

4

You can work two utensils at once if you tape the workpieces together.

5

Cut the doubled-up stack of workpieces at the same time for two identical profiles.

6

Although the handles haven't been shaped yet, a quick sanding refines the profile.

7

A spokeshave quickly roughs out the basic shaping. Be sure the workpiece is secured in a vise or clamp.

With the workpiece still basically square, I find that sanding this face now saves a bit of time later and makes that edge easier to see and follow when cutting the next piece.

Back on the band saw, cut out the second utensil. (**PHOTO 3**)

Although almost the same pattern this second one isn't an exact copy, but rather a sequential copy. For that reason they nest together perfectly atop each other, just as they were originally within the block of wood. For the next few steps let's return them to that state by taping them together, as in **PHOTO 4**.

Transfer the profile pattern to the top of the taped and stacked workpieces, then move over to the band saw again and cut them out at the same time. (**PHOTO 5**)

With the two spatulas still taped,

refine and smooth out the profile on a spindle sander or with a sanding block. Note in **PHOTO 6** that I've taped one side of the stack while I sanded the other. I then swapped the tape and sanded the other side.

SHAPING AND FORMING

Untape the stack and secure a spatula in a vise or clamp it to your workpiece. Begin the rough shaping with a block plane, drawknife or spokeshave, as in **PHOTO 7**. Work your way around the utensil, reclamping and adjusting the position as needed. Don't try to fully form the utensil at this time or you may take off too much material; the idea here is to get the basic shape all around with a blade before refining it with sanding. As you work with the spokeshave, you'll want to switch direction periodically depending on

where the curve puts the end grain.

With everything roughed out, use a disc sander to further shape the convex curves. (**PHOTO 8**) Now move to the spindle sander and work the concave surfaces by simultaneously running the utensil back and forth at the same time you rotate it against the spindle. You'll be surprised at how fast the shaping goes. This sanding is dust intensive, of course, so adequate dust collection for your machines is highly recommended.

When satisfied with the shaping on the machines, switch over to a sanding block and thoroughly go over all surfaces. (**PHOTO 9**) For this phase I started with #80-grit to do the final refining of the shape, then it was just a matter of smoothing, smoothing, smoothing. Progress through #100-, #150- and #220-grit

8

Refine the convex rounded portions on a disc sander. A spindle sander handles the concave curves.

9

Sand with low grits to refine the shape, then move up through the grits for smoothing.

10

Don't toss out the offcuts! There's a host of smaller utensils hiding inside them.

paper on your sanding block, then sand with a folded piece of #220-grit paper to hug the curves. Finally, give everything a good once over with #320-grit for an almost glass-like surface and you're done.

An oil finish works best for hardwood utensils, and really brings out the color of woods like cherry and walnut. I gave mine several coats of boiled linseed oil, allowing 24-36 hours between coats. After the final coat had cured for several days, I went over the utensils with some #400-grit paper and gave them one more coat. After a few more days curing time, a final rubbing out with a crumpled piece of brown paper torn from a grocery bag buffed them to a nice shine.

KEEP 'EM COMING

It's a mantra of mine that there's no such thing as scrap, and making hardwood utensils provides the proof. (**PHOTO 10**) After making two large spatulas and one smaller one, what was left would generally be considered unusable for most other projects because the offcuts are so bizarrely shaped and sized.

For utensils, though, you just keep on cutting the offcuts, making smaller utensils as you go. See that single curved piece in the center of **PHOTO 10** with the loose masking tape? I took the matching piece that was taped to it and made the pot scraper you see at the lower right. That created an even smaller leftover piece, which I turned into the little spreader

just above it. There are two more taped-together pieces here that will yield four more small utensils like these. Meanwhile, I can use those flatter pieces at the top of the photo to make at least four of the Veggie or Pastry Scrapers from two chapters back.

I'd not intended to make those two smaller utensils as part of this project chapter, but decided to go ahead and include both in this chapter's set of patterns.

Enjoy!

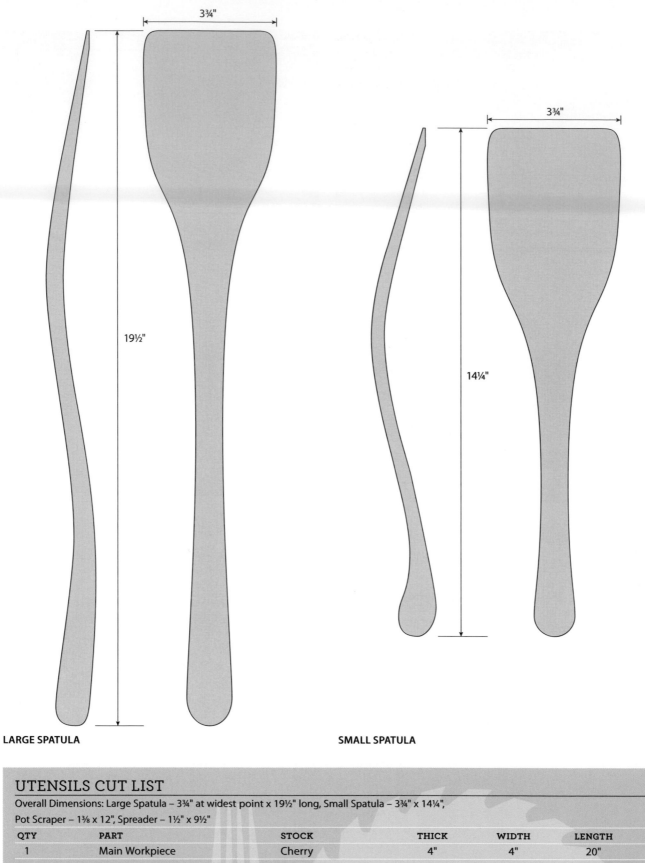

LARGE SPATULA

3¾"

19½"

SMALL SPATULA

3¾"

14¼"

UTENSILS CUT LIST

Overall Dimensions: Large Spatula – 3¾" at widest point x 19½" long, Small Spatula – 3¾" x 14¼",

Pot Scraper – 1⅜ x 12", Spreader – 1½" x 9½"

QTY	PART	STOCK	THICK	WIDTH	LENGTH
1	Main Workpiece	Cherry	4"	4"	20"

NOTES:

Size your workpiece to the type, size and number of utensils you plan to cut from a single piece.

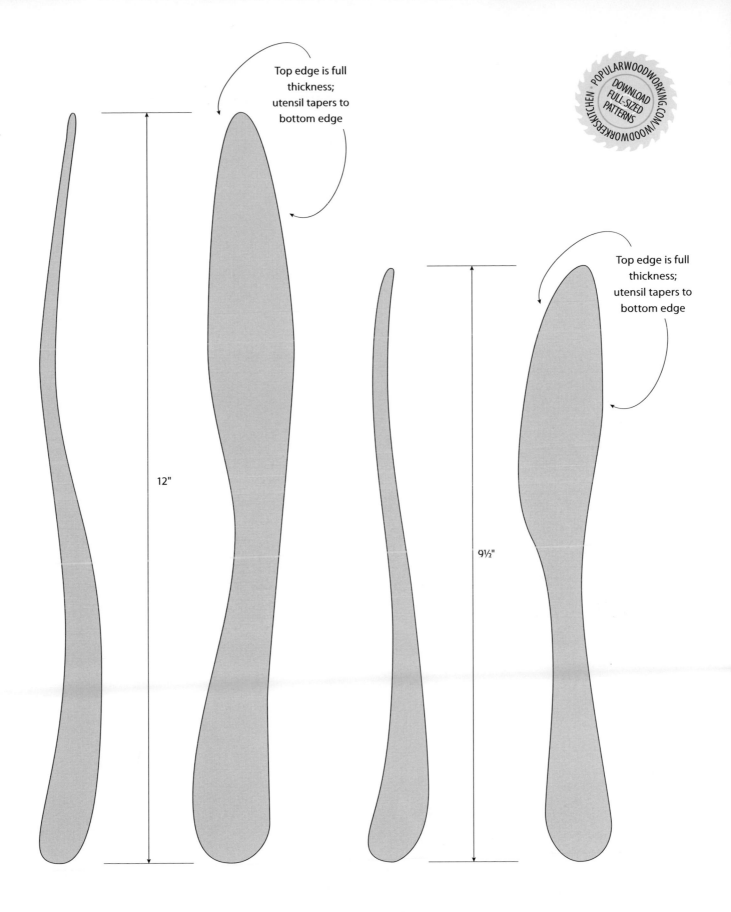

Top edge is full thickness; utensil tapers to bottom edge

12"

Top edge is full thickness; utensil tapers to bottom edge

9½"

DOWNLOAD FULL-SIZED PATTERNS · POPULARWOODWORKING.COM/WOODWORKERSKITCHEN

POT SCRAPER

SPREADER

Trivet

SEVERAL PROJECTS IN THIS book could easily go in more than one section because they serve more than one purpose. The Paper Towel Holder project in the last section, in fact, could fit in all four. Likewise, the trivet presented here does double duty around our house with both meal prep and protecting surfaces in the kitchen and dining room. We've even used it as a protective base for a large vase of flowers from time to time. Without a doubt, it's a bona fide multitasker.

I like the complimentary colors of oak and walnut, but you can make this out of anything. You also don't have to contrast the colors and could instead make this with a single wood species if you'd like. Also, since this isn't a food-contact item, it doesn't matter if the wood is open- or closed-grain. In addition to varying the wood used, feel free to resize this any way you like. If asked, I'd consider this one to be medium, as I could certainly see a use for both smaller and larger versions.

SET IT, FORGET IT

While the lengths of the long slats and spacers are obviously different, everything in this project is the same width so cutting the components goes quickly – if you're using a table saw just set the fence one time, and churn out several long strips for both the long slats and spacers. (**PHOTO 1**)

For cutting parts to length you can use any kind of hand or power saw. On the table saw, swap your fence for a miter gauge to cut all the components to length. For the long slats I used the stop on the miter gauge to turn out identical lengths, but the spacers are too short to be cut safely in this manner. Instead, in **PHOTO 2** you can see how I've put a magnetic stop (actually, the back edge of a magnetic feather board) the proper length from the blade to repeatedly turn out the 1½"-long spacers. The magnetic stop is offset ahead of the blade a couple inches, so there's no

With the fence set, cutting is straightforward since all the components are the same width.

Cut the spacer blocks to length. An offset stop on the saw table helps make the repeat cuts.

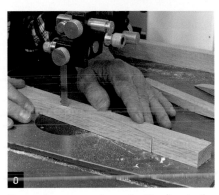

Cut out the curve on the underside of each of the long slats.

danger of getting the part trapped between the blade and the stop when cutting.

The trivet has plenty of space for air movement between the slats, but I also wanted lateral air movement underneath, so there's a curve on the underside of each slat that helps dissipate heat. Transfer the Trivet Pattern from page 73 to the center of each slat, then cut the curve. In **PHOTO 3** I'm using a band saw, but a jigsaw would handle this task just fine. After cutting, give those curves a good sanding to remove saw marks. A spindle sander is perfect for this, but a sanding block does the trick too.

GLUE-UP AND ASSEMBLY

This trivet is small enough to be clamped up as a unit, but I found it easier to do the glue-up in sections. Apply glue to the spacers and sandwich them between the slats to create three subassemblies that are clamped up one at a time. (**PHOTO 4**) Once each subassembly is dry, glue and clamp the three of them together to complete the trivet.

The trivet can be left square on the end, but I decided to add an appealing curve that looks nice and cuts the weight just a bit. The dimensions of the curve aren't critical at all; I just traced it onto the workpiece with a large serving platter. Cut the curve with a band saw or jigsaw, then sand

Apply glue to the spacer blocks and sandwich them in between the slats.

After cutting the curved end, smooth on a disc sander.

A quick trip through the planer levels both the top and bottom surfaces.

Slightly round all the sharp edges with a folded piece of sandpaper.

your saw marks off. (**PHOTO 5**)

Since this is glued up from several pieces, you may need to level the surface. You can do this with sanding or planing. At 11¾" in length the trivet is a bit short for most planers, but it's easy to fool the planer by adding some temporary side pieces of the same thickness with hot-melt glue. These act to "lengthen" the workpiece for planing not only the flat top side, but the ends of the bottom curved side as well. (**PHOTO 6**) After planing, those side guides pop right off.

Give the trivet a thorough sanding all around up to #150-grit. All those slats are going to have pretty sharp edges, so be sure to ease these with a folded piece of sandpaper to slightly round the edges of the wood along each space. (**PHOTO 7**) There are sharp edges on the underside, too, so be sure to do the same sanding there.

Any finish at all works well for your trivet. However, you can certainly count on food getting spilled on it from time to time so my recommendation is a coat or two of polyurethane. I used a wiping varnish that cured quickly and gave the trivet a nice satin sheen.

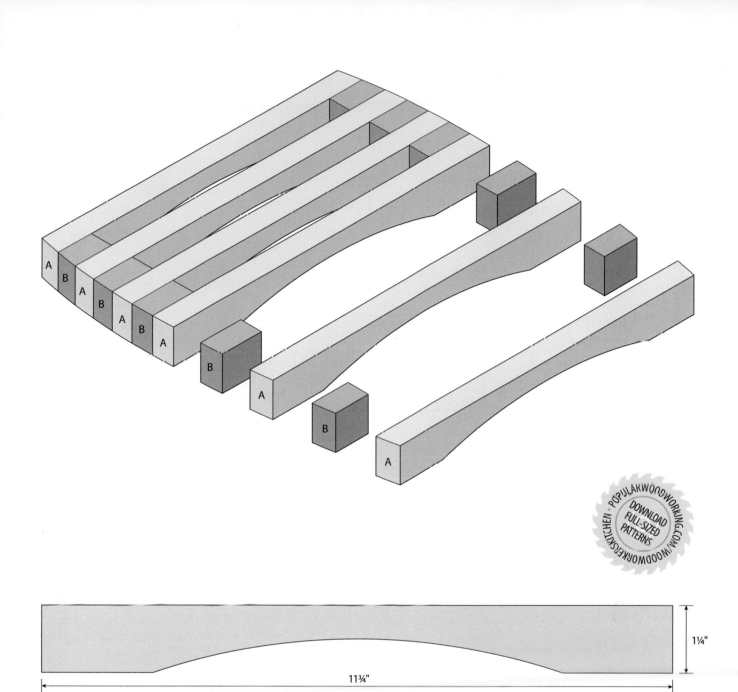

TRIVET PATTERN

11¾"

1¼"

TRIVET CUT LIST

Overall Dimensions: 1¼" x 8¼" x 11¾"

REF	QTY	PART	STOCK	THICKNESS	WIDTH	LENGTH
A	6	Long Slats	Oak	¾"	1¼"	11¾" (a)
B	10	Contrasting Spacers	Walnut	¾"	1¼"	1½" (a)

NOTES:

(a) Working length is listed above; final length will change once finished trivet is shaped.

SERVING

✦

THE STOVE AND OVEN ARE OFF, KNIVES AND UTENSILS ARE
put away, the whole house is filled with the aroma of good cooking, and
the meal is ready. ✦ And whether it's for your family, a dining room full
of family and friends, or just an intimate dinner for two, serving a home-
cooked meal is often the most pleasurable part of the cooking process.
Not only do you get to show off your work (just like with a project from
your workshop), but it adds an entirely literal meaning to
making a project with "good taste."

✦

Cheese Board

WHEN I WAS IN ELEMENTARY
school, I was always fascinated with the paper cutter. We were never allowed to use it, of course, because we might cut ourselves, but the way it worked just amazed me at the time. Danger aside, to the little kid in me they looked like a lot of fun to use. You can imagine my sense of déjà vu the first time I saw a cheese slicer of the type presented in this chapter, and it's not surprising why – they function exactly the same way as those paper cutters. But the results of their work are a lot tastier.

Wire-based cheese cutters have been around forever, but most are handheld and require a separate cutting surface. Then someone – I have no idea who – came up with the idea of taking the wire from those handheld cutters and combining them with the same mechanism that made paper cutters work so well. The results are attractive, useful and, dare I say it, fun to use.

The heart of the cutter is a thin piece of wire attached to a heavier U-shaped wire handle. When assembled the wire should be taut so bringing the handle down cleanly slices the cheese. It's like a little paper cutter or, for that matter, a tiny miter saw for the culinary set.

GET STARTED
Before getting to work you'll need to acquire an inexpensive cheese wire slicer kit, available from most woodworking suppliers and a number of sources online. Sizes vary slightly, but whatever kit you get will give the appropriate dimensions and distances for construction for that particular model.

The kit I got uses a board measuring 5¾" in width (determined by the size of the U-shaped handle). The length of the board doesn't matter, so I settled for an even 10". This is a food-contact item, so you'll want to use a close-grain hardwood for the board. Once again, I opted to use some more of that figured maple you've seen in a few projects here already.

Cut the base for the cheese board to size.

Drill a ¼" hole in the end of the board to accept the end of the pivoting wire hardware.

Cut a ⅜"-deep slot across what will be the top surface of the board to act as a recess for the cutter wire.

Cut the board to size by your preferred means. (**PHOTO 1**) Remember, although the length can be variable, you must use the width specified by the manufacturer of the wire kit.

One end of the U-shaped handle fits into a ¼" hole drilled lengthwise through the rear edge of the board. Without a means of drilling vertically, such as on a drill press, this can be a little difficult, but I've come up with a trick for doing it without a drill press.

Most cordless drills rest flat on their sides, and if yours does you're in luck. To drill a perfectly vertical hole, all you need is to hold the drill securely flat on your workbench or other work surface. Now, with a little bit of trial and error you can support the workpiece such that the desired drilling spot is level with the horizontal bit. For my drill, a piece of ¾" plywood was the perfect thickness to accomplish this as you can see in **PHOTO 2**. For your drill, try differing thickness of wood or other material to support your workpiece; some combination is sure to work just fine.

Drill the handle hole in the location and to the depth specified by your cheese wire kit. For mine the hole needed to be 5" from the front of the board and drilled to a depth of 3⅞".

In use, the cutter wire needs to go cleanly all the way through the cheese, and this is accomplished by cutting a recess slot on the top of the board where the wire falls. (**PHOTO 3**) Again, your wire kit will determine the location and depth of the slot,

Round over all the top and bottom edges of the board.

When sanding the board, be sure to also sand the sharp edges of the wire slot.

Hold the cutter wire's loop end at the front of the slot, and slip the cutting hardware into place through the side hole and into the loop.

Fold the handle knob back to tighten the wire, and secure with a screw.

but most likely it will be around 3" from the end of the board where you drilled the hole and ⅜" deep. Be sure to keep the board oriented so the cut is in the correct relation to the handle hole – it'd be easy to inadvertently flip the board the wrong way.

FINISHING AND ASSEMBLY

You can leave the board edges square if you like, but I decided to add a full bullnose to all four edges with a roundover bit in my router table, as in **PHOTO 4**. I first did all four bottom edges, then flipped the board over and did all four top edges.

Give the board a thorough sanding all around. I like as smooth a surface as possible for food-contact items to minimize the chances of food lodging in the wood, so I sanded

up to #220-grit on this cheese board. When sanding, be sure to ease the sharp edges on the wire recess slot by going back and forth over both edges with a piece of folded sandpaper, as in **PHOTO 5**. Not only does this look nicer and feel good to the touch, but with those edges rounded slightly the wire will have less of a tendency to catch on the sides of the slot.

It'll be easier to finish the board now before we tackle assembly. As with the Sink Board project earlier, I applied several coats of thinned Danish oil, an oil/varnish blend. After each coat was fully cured I gave the board a light once-over with #400-grit sandpaper.

When your finishing job is fully dry, begin assembly by removing the knob and its attached wire from the

U-shaped handle. Note that there is a small hole on this end of the handle for the set screw; the pivot end does not have this hole. Hold the loop on the end of the wire down into the back of the slot where your drilled hole crosses, then slide the pivot side of the wire handle into the hole and through the loop where it crosses the slot, capturing the wire on that end. (**PHOTO 6**)

Slide the knob back onto the other end of the handle, then angle and snap it into place so the wire is taut, making sure the hole in the knob lines up with the set screw hole in the handle. Now, just insert the set screw and tighten it in place, as in **PHOTO 7**.

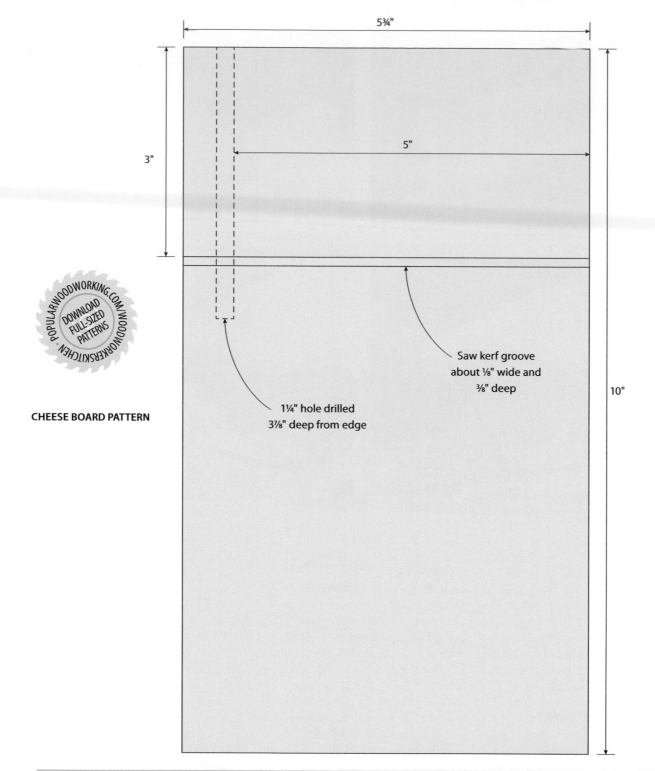

5¾"

5"

3"

10"

POPULARWOODWORKING.COM/WOODWORKERSKITCHEN
DOWNLOAD FULL-SIZED PATTERNS

CHEESE BOARD PATTERN

1¼" hole drilled
3⅞" deep from edge

Saw kerf groove
about ⅛" wide and
⅜" deep

CHEESE BOARD CUT LIST
Overall Dimensions: ¾" x 5¾" x 10"

QTY	PART	STOCK	THICKNESS	WIDTH	LENGTH
1	Main Board	Maple	¾"	5¾"	10"

ADDITIONAL MATERIALS:
Cheese Wire Kit

Bread Knife

THERE'S NOTHING AT ALL
wrong with an ordinary bread knife
– I have one in my knife block right
now, in fact – but they are, well, ordinary. But just as the smooth curves of
the wooden spatulas in the hardwood
Utensils project in the previous section are nicer than ordinary spatulas,
so, too, are wooden bread knives. And
for all the same reasons.

These knives are often called bow
knives because they look, and function, just like a violin bow or a bow
saw. Made of the hardwood of your
choice, they're an attractive addition
to any table, and they make excellent
gifts.

We'll take a two-part look at options with these knives in the next
two projects, but in this chapter let's
concentrate on making the knife
itself.

While you'll obviously be cutting bread with it, you won't literally
prepare food on it in a typical food-
contact way (only the blade touches
the food), so any hardwood is fine.
I've elected to use red oak, but cherry,
walnut or any other strong hardwood
would be a good choice.

Before getting started you'll need
to purchase a bread blade, but they're
easy to find through any woodworking supplier. There's little difference
among the brands out there, but
always measure the one you get and
adjust project parameters and drilling
locations accordingly.

MAKE THE KNIFE HANDLE
Transfer the handle shape from the
Bread Knife Pattern on page 81. You
can either trace the pattern directly
onto the wood, or photocopy, cut out
and adhere it to the wood with spray
adhesive or contact cement as I've
opted to do in **PHOTO 1**. Cut out the
handle following the pattern on the
band saw as shown here, or with a
jigsaw or even a scrollsaw. By hand,
a coping saw may be slow but could
also handle the task.

Refine and smooth the handle
shape by sanding. A disc sander
makes fast work of all the convex

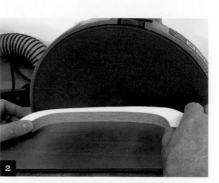

Cut out the knife profile with a band saw,
jigsaw, scrollsaw or coping saw.

Refine the convex surfaces of the knife profile
on the disc sander, or by hand with a sanding
block.

A spindle sander excels at smoothing the
concave portions of the knife handle.

Mark the handle for the blade screw locations.

surfaces, as in **PHOTO 2**, but you can
also use a sanding block. Since we'll
be routing the handle at a later point,
there's no need to go higher than
#100-grit paper here.

For the inside of the bow and the
concave portion of the handle, you
can't beat a spindle sander. (**PHOTO
3**) Again, sanding just to #100-grit is
fine for now.

Tape the blade in place across the
bow opening so that the business
edge of the blade is flush with what
will be the bottom of the bow. In
PHOTO 4, I have it oriented for my
own right-handed use, but for left-
ies the blade should be flush on the
other side. Use an awl or other sharp
tool to mark the screw holes in the
blade right through the tape. Notice
here that I'm doing two things to
avoid cutting myself on the blade.
The first is clamping the handle
bow-up securely to my workbench,
and the other is wearing a thick glove
that allows me to handle the blade
directly without worry.

Remove the taped blade and set
it aside, but leave the handle secured
to the bench. We want the blade to
be under slight tension so it's taut in
use. To accomplish this, drill one of
the pilot holes exactly on your mark.
The second one, however, should be
drilled about 1⁄16" to 3⁄32" outside your
mark.

Drive the holding screw on one
side of the blade just far enough so it
stays securely in the pilot hole. Now,
insert the other screw through the
blade and into the pilot hole on the
opposite end. It'll fight you a little
since it's a bit farther away, and you
may need to flex the bow a bit, but
it should go in with no problem.
Tighten the screw down all the way
on that side, and then go back to the
other side and do the same. (**PHOTO
5**) Once again, I'd wear gloves while
doing this.

SHAPE AND FINISH THE HANDLE
Remove the screws and blade temporary and set them aside in a safe

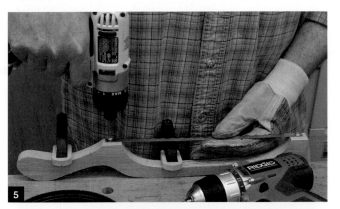

Drill pilot holes – slightly offset on one side to keep the blade taut – and screw the blade into place.

With the blade removed, give all edges of the knife handle a roundover on the router table.

place. Be sure not to lose the screws.

Round over all edges of the knife handle except the two flat spots where the blade attaches. A ⅜" roundover bit in a router table works well for this task. (**PHOTO 6**) I wanted the knife to still have a more-or-less square profile in cross section, so I've set the bit slightly low in the table to leave flat surfaces on all but the thinnest portions of the bow.

Now, give the handle a good sanding all around up to #150-grit, then apply the finish of your choice. I went with a simple boiled linseed oil finish, and applied three coats. After the final coat, I went over the handle with a crumpled piece of brown paper bag to buff the surface to a light sheen. If you prefer a bit more shine and protection, a wipe-on polyurethane finish would be a good choice.

When the finish has cured reattach the blade, head into the kitchen and start baking bread.

15¾"

2¼"

BREAD KNIFE CUT LIST
Overall Dimensions: ¾" x 3¼" x 15¾"

QTY	PART	STOCK	THICK	WIDTH	LENGTH
1	Main Workpiece	Oak	¾"	2¼"	15¾"

ADDITIONAL MATERIALS:
Bread Knife Blade w/ Mounting Screws
Blade Guard Sleeve

SAFELY STORING YOUR KNIFE

Let me say this right here: These blades are really sharp, and unlike an ordinary bread knife that can be slipped into a knife block when not in use, this will likely be stored in a drawer or cupboard. With that in mind the blade should be protected when not in use to prevent accidental cuts.

Knife blade covers are commercially available, but not that easy to find except through kitchen suppliers. Covers for woodworking handsaw blades can also be had. However, both those options are, in my opinion, pricier than they should be, plus you might need to special order them.

An easy alternative can be found at any office supply store. Pick up a package of report covers, those clear plastic folders that hold several sheets of paper. These come with plastic spines that snap onto the edge of the cover to hold the pages in place and a package of six costs about $3.

Just trim the spine to length with shears or a utility knife, and then slip it over the edge of the knife blade. The spring-like cover grabs and stays on the blade nicely, and the bright colors (except for the black ones) are a visible warning that a sharp blade is hiding inside.

The snap-on spine from a report cover from an office supply store makes a perfect blade guard for this knife.

Bread Board Combo

IN THIS SECOND OF OUR TWO part look at bread knives, we'll combine a knife like the one from the previous chapter with its own cutting board. The board does double duty, providing both a cutting surface and built-in storage for the knife. When the knife is nestled into its matching nook in the board, the sharp edge is contained safely on the inside.

The knife here is identical to the earlier one, but where that one was cut from a workpiece just large enough for the knife pattern, this one is "lifted" from the center of a larger board to create a matching cutout to store it in. Since the construction of the knife is the same as the one in the previous project, we'll skip most of that procedure this time around.

You can use any wood you like for the knife and the cutout side of the board since they're not food-contact items. For the cutting board side, use only a closed-grain hardwood. You can make the entire board out of the same closed-grain species if you want, but I opted once again for the oak/walnut contrast I enjoy so much – oak for the knife and holder, walnut for the cutting surface.

As always, adjust the size of the main board any way you like. My wife and I love Italian and French bread so a narrower board suited my needs, but widen the board all you want.

By the way, keep in mind that this is a right-handed knife and board – you want the business edge of the blade oriented down into the cutout when stored, therefore the knife points to the left. To orient a left-handed knife blade downward, glue up the board so the cutout points in the opposite direction.

CREATE THE CUTOUT

Cut the main workpiece and the cutting surface to size. Set the cutting surface aside for now and transfer the knife pattern from page 81 in the previous chapter to the center of the main workpiece with the blade portion parallel to one edge. Consider the blade location your cut line, ex-

Transfer the handle pattern to the main workpiece, then cut along the knife line.

tend it to the ends, then slice off the bottom portion of the workpiece, as in **PHOTO 1**. With the offcut butted up to the rest of the board at the cut line, pencil in some marks across the cut to act as a guide for reassembly, then set the offcut aside for now.

Cut the handle out (**PHOTO 2**), taking care to follow the pattern exactly and in a single motion – no stopping, backing up, correcting, etc. – so the handle comes out cleanly. (In the previous chapter since everything but the handle itself was just small offcuts, we didn't have to worry about this.)

At this point, all instructions for the bread knife itself are identical to the one in the last chapter, so we won't repeat them here. Complete the knife per those instructions, and then continue with the board.

ASSEMBLY

Put the smaller curved center piece in a safe place – we'll get to it later – and apply glue to the cut edges of the board, making sure your marks are aligned. Clamp up till dry. (**PHOTO 3**)

Thoroughly sand the inside surface of the cutout to smooth and refine the opening. A spindle sander is great for the curved portions, while a sanding block works well on the flat spots. Check the knife fit in the opening occasionally as you work,

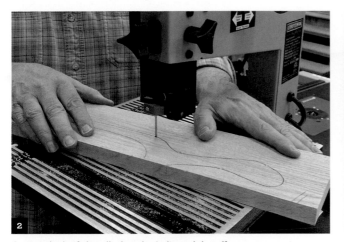

Cut out the knife handle, but don't discard the offcuts.

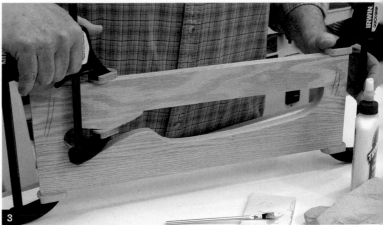

Glue the outer portion of the board back together, making sure to line up your marks.

Apply glue to the back face of the reconstructed main workpiece.

Clamp up the assembly and allow to dry.

and refine the opening as needed with a bit more sanding if the knife fits too snugly inside the opening. I've done the one here so that the original band saw kerf plus sanding gave me a gap of about ⅛" all around. Also at this time, level the back surface in preparation for gluing by sanding or a quick run through a planer.

Spread glue on the back of the main workpiece, as in **PHOTO 4**. When the glue is applied, flip it onto the cutting surface. Note here that those few blemishes on the one side of the walnut are no problem – they'll be hidden inside the completed board once glued up.

Clamp up the assembly till dry.

(**PHOTO 5**) Since you cut both workpieces to the same working size, the cutting surface will be slightly larger than the main workpiece (the kerf from that first cut removed ⅛" in width), so trim the sides and ends as needed to flush the surfaces all around. (**PHOTO 6**)

You can leave the board squared if you like, but I decided to round the four corners on the band saw, and then give all the top and bottom edges a roundover on the router table, as in **PHOTO 7**. The ⅜" roundover bit I'm using here exactly matches the ⅜" thickness of the cutting surface, so the rounded portion meets the main board right at the joint.

Now, grab that smaller center piece from when we cut out the knife handle, and place it and the knife in the board opening. (This is easier if you remove the blade.) A narrow piece of ⅛"-thick scrap serves as a good spacer for the setting the gap on the blade side of the handle. (**PHOTO 8**) If everything fits correctly, apply glue to the underside of that center piece, then glue and clamp it into place.

When dry, give the entire board a good sanding up to at least #150-grit. As in earlier projects, since this is a food-contact item I took the sanding up to #220-grit on the walnut cutting surface.

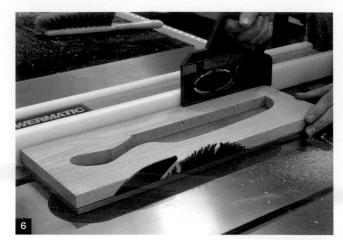

6 Trim the edges of the bread board assembly as needed after removing the clamps.

7 Round off the corners, then give the top and bottom edges a roundover on the router table.

Apply the finish of your choice to protect the board and make the wood grain pop, as in **PHOTO 9**. I used boiled linseed oil, but a thinned oil/varnish blend would also be a good pick.

One of the things I like best about this board is that everything on the knife side was cut from a single piece of wood. This means that once assembled, this side of the bread board has continuous grain that runs from one side to the other, even flowing right through the knife handle.

8

Use the knife handle and a thin strip of scrap to locate the center piece before gluing it into place.

9

Give the completed bread board the finish of your choice.

BREAD BOARD CUT LIST

Overall Dimensions: 1⅜" x 6⅜" x 19"

QTY	PART	STOCK	THICKNESS	WIDTH	LENGTH
1	Main Workpiece	Oak	¾"	6½"	19"
1	Cutting Surface	Walnut	⅜"	6½"	19"

NOTE:
Although Part A is 6½" wide, it loses ⅛" when cut in the middle, creating the final project width of 6⅜"

ADDITIONAL MATERIALS:
Bread Knife Blade w/ Mounting Screws

16

Spring Tongs

GETTING SPRING-LIKE ACTION
on any articulated utensil generally requires some sort of added hardware, usually metal. But with careful shaping of two workpieces you can also generate just enough tension that a springing action is created whenever the two pieces are in the correct position. That's the case with these serving tongs.

With a pivot on one end, each half is free to swing a full 180° each way. Fold them in one direction and the raised portion of the fingers"in the back press against each other to create the springy pressure that forces them open, a perfect trait for serving tongs. But fold them in the opposite direction and the raised portions of the fingers are oriented outward and the two halves rest completely flat against each other.

Hardwood is a must for these tongs, and since they're food handling items a closed-grain species is best. I've used walnut for the project tongs (and maple for the smaller set in the opening photo), but cherry, birch or another closed-grain hardwood is fine.

SHAPE THE HALVES

Cut your workpieces to size. (**PHOTO 1**) Once shaped, the tong halves are only ½" thick at the widest part, but it's best to use stock of at least ¾" thick for the resawing process in the next step. You can get two tong halves out of a single piece of 11" stock, but it may be difficult – the first one is fairly straightforward as the ¾" workpiece is easy to keep vertical as you saw, but once cut the remainder is thinner and may be harder to resaw. If you have any doubts, use two pieces of ¾" stock to create your tong halves.

Transfer the Spring Tongs Pattern from page 91 to the edge of your workpiece, and cut out the first tong half on the band saw, as in **PHOTO 2**. Although it's possible to cut out by hand, a band saw is really the tool of choice for this task. Now, cut out the second tong half from the remainder

Cut your workpieces to overall size.

Resaw the workpieces per the pattern to create the two halves of the tongs.

Use a sanding block to remove saw marks and level the surface smooth.

(the raised portion would be at the other end) or from a fresh piece of ¾" stock.

By the way, at this point the two halves are identical. We'll trim them later so that the finger ends are different, but for now you can work with them interchangeably.

Use a sanding block to remove saw marks and smooth the sawn flat portions and rounded ends. (**PHOTO 3**)

Referring once again to the pattern, transfer the cut lines for the fingers to the raised end of each tong half. On the pattern, I've set the cut lines so the center finger is exactly ½" wide. The width of the outer fingers will depend on the kerf of your saw blade. However, with the center finger a uniform ½" in width, the exact

width of the outer ones isn't critical.

Set up your band saw fence to make a cut to create that ½" center finger, then clamp a piece of scrap to act as a stop so all your cuts will be of identical depth. Run the finger end of each tong through the blade and up to the stop, and then flip it over and repeat the cut, as in **PHOTO 4**.

MAKE IT SPRING

To create the spring action, the ends of the two halves must be trimmed differently to work in concert. Using the pattern as a guide once again, cut 1⅝" off the ends of the two outer fingers on one tong half.

Now, remove the center finger from the other half altogether. This is easily done by simply drilling at the

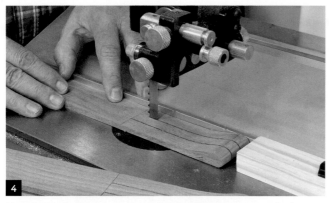

Mark the cut lines on the two tong halves and cut on your marks. A stop block helps make exactly equal cuts.

Trim the outer pieces of one tong half, and remove the center finger from the other.

Drill a ³⁄₁₆" hole in the assembled tongs for the pivot dowel.

Taper the outer tips of the tong ends as desired.

base of the finger, as in **PHOTO 5**. The size of the drill you'll need depends on your saw's kerf and the resulting width of the outer fingers. The idea is that you want a hole that equals the distance between the two outer fingers, so the drill bit will be ½" plus whatever the thickness of both kerfs is. Just measure exactly between the two outer fingers, and choose a drill bit of that size.

Put the two halves together in the flat folded orientation. Depending on your cuts and earlier sanding, those two short outer fingers may not fit exactly flush against the opposite tong where it starts to get thicker at the raised end. If this is the case, just sand the ends where they touch until it's a flush fit and the two halves fit nice and flat against each other.

Tape the two halves together and drill a ³⁄₁₆" hole through the center of the raised ends, as in **PHOTO 6**. Note here that I've clamped the assembled and taped tongs to a block that I know to be square to ensure a perfectly vertical hole all the way through.

Give the outside tips a slight taper. I'm using a disc sander in **PHOTO 7**, but you can also do this quickly with a sanding block. Be sure you're creating the taper on the outer face — the same face with the raised portions. If you taper the inner faces the two tips won't meet when using the tongs to pick up something.

With the pivot dowel inserted, you can see how the two halves fit together.

Apply glue to the end of the dowel and slide it into place.

Give everything a good sanding up to at least #150-grit. (I went to #220 for a really smooth surface.) Use a folded piece of sandpaper to smooth the insides of the kerf cuts between the fingers. Also, round over the ends of those two shortened fingers.

Reassemble the tongs and insert a short length of ³⁄₁₆" hardwood dowel into the pivot hole you drilled and check all clearances and the working action. In **PHOTO 8**, you can see how I've rounded the tips of the two shorter fingers and how the two halves fit flush in the folded position.

To permanently mount the pivot dowel you want glue on only the outer ends to allow the tongs to pivot freely. Slide the dowel through the hole one side until it just enters the hole on the far side. Dab a bit of glue into the hole on the far side, and a bit on the shaft of the dowel just before it enters on the near side, as in **PHOTO 9**. You don't need much at all so go sparingly with the glue. Push the dowel home until it just clears the far side, and then wipe off excess glue – you'll have squeeze-out on both sides. When the glue has dried, trim the dowel on both sides and sand flush.

Give your tongs the oil finish of your choice. I gave the project tongs two coats of boiled linseed oil, which I buffed to a nice sheen once cured.

This is a great project to customize by just altering the size of the tongs to fit whatever task you have in mind for them. The 11" ones here work great for salad, while the 8" maple ones in the opening photo are perfect for veggies and snacks. A larger pair with thicker tong halves would be great for using on the grill, or you could make a pair just for using with a skillet on the stove.

SPRING TONGS CUT LIST

Overall Dimensions: ½" x 1¾" x 11"

QTY	PART	STOCK	THICKNESS	WIDTH	LENGTH
1	Center Section	Walnut	½"	1¾"	11"
1	Outer Section	Walnut	½"	1¾"	11"
1	Pivot Pin	Hardwood Dowel	³⁄₁₆"	n/a	1¾"

NOTES:
Any hardwood may be used, but closed-grain is best. Pivot dowel can be matching or contrasting species.

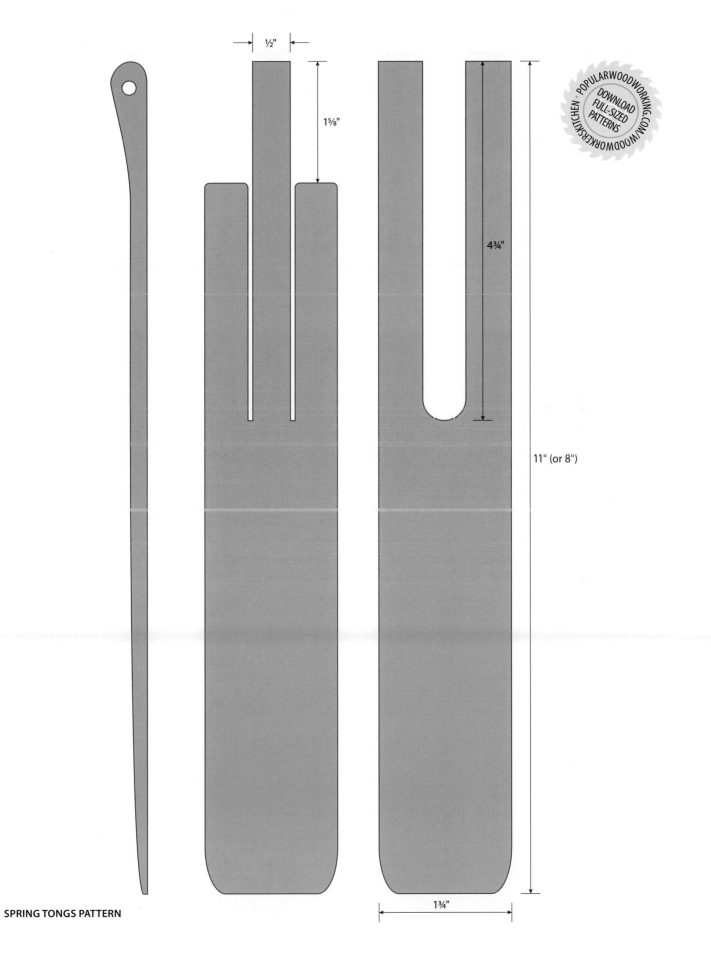

½"

1⅝"

4¾"

11" (or 8")

1¾"

DOWNLOAD FULL-SIZED PATTERNS

POPULARWOODWORKING.COM/WOODWORKERSKITCHEN

SPRING TONGS PATTERN

Cruet Server

WHETHER EATEN AS A SNACK, a first course, a side dish or as the entire meal, who doesn't love a great salad? Of course, a salad's only as good as the dressing that goes atop it, and the range of tastes for that are all over the board. My usual favorites are ranch and honey mustard, but sometimes I like to go back to basics with a simple oil-and-vinegar dressing poured and then combined right on the salad. Add some salt and freshly ground pepper, and I'm in heaven.

At the dinner table, the best way to serve up oil and vinegar is from a matched set of cruets. Include a holder designed specifically for them, and they're easy to pass around the table. For storage, the whole thing stashes away in a cabinet, or can be left out as an attractive kitchen accent.

I have several other dinner pieces in cherry and so that's what I've selected here, but walnut, maple, oak or any other hardwood would also be a good choice. Keep in mind that all the dimensions – particularly the large holes drilled for the base and holder workpieces – are based on the glass bottles I used. Adjust yours accordingly to accommodate the bottles you find.

DOUBLE IT UP

There are only two main wooden components to create, a ¾"-thick base and a ¼"-thick bottle holder mounted above the base. Although different in thickness, these components are the same size and shape, and share drilled holes in the same places. For that reason, you'll find the project goes faster and more efficiently by working the two pieces at the same time.

Cut these two pieces to size by your preferred method. (**PHOTO 1**) The table saw is a good choice, as you can leave your setups the same for each piece to assure the workpieces come out identical.

Stack the thinner bottle holder atop the base workpiece, orienting the presentation faces upward, and wrap tape around the stack to hold

1

Cut the base and bottle holder to the same width and length on the table saw.

2

With the base and bottle holder stacked, taped and marked, cut the rounded ends on the band saw.

3

Refine the rounded ends and smooth out the band saw marks with a disc sander or sanding block.

the pieces tightly together. With them doubled-up you can work them simultaneously in the coming steps for identical results.

Round each end of the stack per the Cruet Pattern on page 96 with a band saw, as in **PHOTO 2**, or a jigsaw or scrollsaw.

Move over to the disc sander to smooth out the end curves. (**PHOTO 3**) Keep in mind that hardwoods like cherry and maple tend to burn when power sanded, so keep the workpiece moving and use only a light pressure as you sand.

With the stack still taped, drill the bottle holes. My bottles have a diameter of 2", so I've mounted a 2⅛" Forstner bit in my drill press. (Be

sure to size your bit to accommodate the bottles you plan to use.) Set the depth stop so that it will drill the stack all the way through the thinner bottle holder and ⅜" into the base, and then drill the first bottle hole, as in **PHOTO 4**. Flip the stack around and drill the other end.

Remove the Forstner bit and replace it with a ⁵⁄₁₆" bit to drill the center hole for the post tenon. Drill both pieces in the stack as before, but this time set the depth stop so the bit just barely goes into the base. The idea here is to drill cleanly through the bottle holder on top of the stack, but only mark the base enough to act as a visible drilling location for the next step.

With the ⁵⁄₁₆" tenon hole drilled,

With the parts still stacked, drill bottle holes in each end; the holes go all the way through the holder, but extend only ⅜" into the base piece.

Drill a ⁵⁄₁₆" hole ¾" deep into the top of the base post. Do the same thing for the bottom of the handle post.

Glue the post tenon dowel into the top of the base post.

With the base post glued into the base, glue the bottle holder in place over the post tenon.

Remove any stamped markings from the top of the copper cap and smooth the edge of the open end with #150-grit sandpaper.

Cut thin cork discs and glue them into the bottle holes in the base. A wooden toy wheel makes a nice clamping caul.

untape your stack and set the bottle holder aside for now. Chuck up a ¾" bit and, using the mark created in the previous step as a guide, drill a ¾" hole ½" deep into the center of the base.

The next step with these two components is assembly, so now's the time to give both a good sanding up to #220-grit. Hand sanding with a sanding block works best for all the exterior surfaces; for the inside of the bottle holder holes a spindle sander is a good choice, but by hand with a folded piece of sandpaper is fine.

HANDLE POST AND ASSEMBLY

Prepare the center post by cutting sections of a ¾" cherry dowel to 2¾" for the base post, and 5" for the handle post. Mark the centers of these two pieces on the cut faces between them, keeping the grain orientation intact – you'll want to grain-match the center post when assembled.

Drill a ⁵⁄₁₆" hole ¾" deep in the top of the base post and a matching hole in the bottom of the handle post. A simple vertical-drilling jig like the one in **PHOTO 5** is the best method to do this. The jig is simply two small pieces of wood joined at a right angle, which in turn is attached to a longer base. The right angle in the center allows you to clamp dowels, rods and other workpieces into place for drilling, ensuring perfectly vertical holes.

Cut a 1¾" tenon, used to join the two post pieces, from a ⁵⁄₁₆" hardwood dowel. The combined depth of the two holes in the posts plus the hole in the bottle holder comes to 1¾", and if the holes you drilled in the posts are spot-on, this will be perfect. However, do a quick dry assembly to check clearances. If the post holes are shallow there may be a gap where the posts join in the center. Trim or sand the post tenon to shorten it until the gap disappears.

For the assembly itself, glue the post tenon into the top of the base post. (**PHOTO 6**) Now, glue the base post into the ¾" hole in the base.

Apply glue to the top of the base post and slip the bottle holder into place. In **PHOTO 7,** you can see how I'm using the flat surface of my workbench to align the two pieces.

While this base/bottle holder subassembly is drying, prepare the finial cap for the handle. I've made this finial out of an ordinary ¾" copper plumbing cap, but when polished it adds the perfect finishing touch and a positive grip to the completed cruet server. There's probably a number or other marking stamped on top, so start your sanding there by rubbing the cap over a sheet of #150-grit paper on a flat surface, as in **PHOTO 8.** When the top is smooth and blemish free, sand the open edge smooth, then follow by sanding the whole surface with increasingly higher grits till it's as smooth and shiny as you can get it. Finally, continue the polishing with increasingly finer steel wool till you bring it to a nice shine.

The cap is mounted atop the handle post by simply gluing it into place with epoxy. Mix up a small batch of epoxy according to package directions and dab it into the cap. Despite the nominal ¾" size of the cap it'll be slightly larger than the ¾" handle post, so you'll need about ¼ to ½ teaspoon or so. Press the top of the handle post into the cap – the glue will flow up around it – and allow the epoxy to cure.

Apply glue into the hole at the bottom of the handle post and twist it into place atop the base/bottle holder subassembly. While the glue is still fresh, twist the handle post so the grain aligns with grain on the base post.

When the completed assembly is dry, apply the finish of your choice. I wanted a bit of shine to this project plus some protection against spilled vinegar and oil, so I opted for a polyurethane wiping varnish. I applied two coats, and when dry rubbed it out lightly with fine steel wool for an even sheen.

The bottoms of the bottle holes in the base probably look a bit rough, so let's dress them up with a thin cork coaster insert. This provides an attractively textured look, and adds a firm but slightly cushioned surface for the bottles to sit on.

You'll find rolls of thin cork (usually about 3/32" thick) at any craft store. Use a compass to draw a pair of circles matching the size of the base holes and cut them out with scissors. Now just glue them into place inside the base holes. In **PHOTO 9** I'm using some conveniently sized wooden toy wheels as clamping cauls to prevent the cork discs from curling up before the glue dries, but any small disk or scrap will work fine.

Now all that's left is to fill the bottles with your favorite oil and vinegar.

And make a salad, of course.

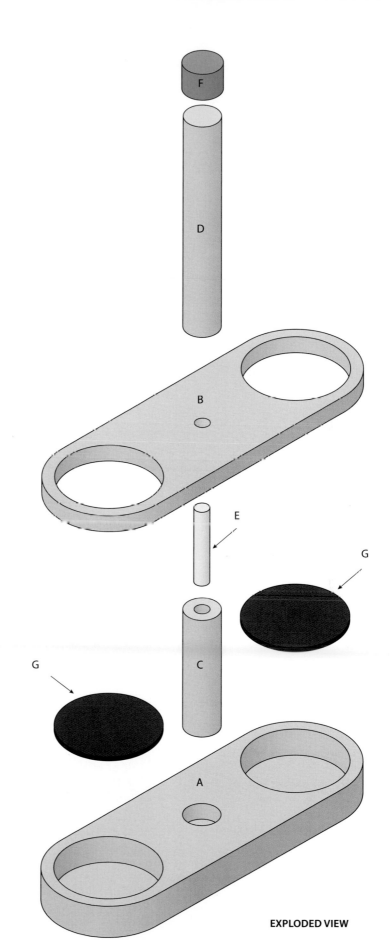

EXPLODED VIEW

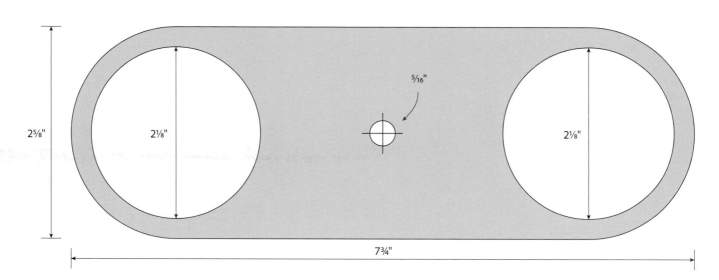

2⅝"

2⅛"

5/16"

2⅛"

7¾"

CRUET PATTERN

CRUET SERVER CUT LIST

Overall Dimensions: 2⅝" x 7¾" x 8⅜" (height includes copper cap)

REF	QTY	PART	STOCK	THICKNESS	WIDTH	LENGTH
A	1	Base	Cherry	¾"	2⅝"	7¾"
B	1	Bottle Holder	Cherry Dowel	⅜"	2⅝"	7¾"
C	1	Base Post	Cherry Dowel	¾"	---	2¾"
D	1	Handle Post	Cherry Dowel	¾"	---	5"
E	1	Post Tenon	Harwood Dowel	5/16"	---	1¾" (a)
F	1	Handle Finial	Copper Cap (b)	---	---	---
G	2	Coaster Insert	Cork Disc	3/32" (c)	---	2⅛"

NOTES:

(a) 1¾" is the nominal length of the post tenon; trim or sand it to slightly less to allow adequate clearance during assembly

(b) Part F is a standard ¾" copper plumbing cap

(c) Thickness may vary depending on source

Napkin Rings

I LOVE WOODEN BOXES, AND one of my favorite types to make is constructed from a single block of wood. These are often called band saw boxes because that's the most common way they're made. It's the band saw's extremely thin blade, in fact, that makes them possible – a table saw's wide kerf creates such a gap that rejoining the grain afterward is often quite visible. The hallmark of these boxes is that the grain is continuous throughout the finished project. You can see a perfect example at right.

These are constructed by cutting apart a solid block of wood in a specific order while carefully tracking each part (marking them is a must), then removing whatever inner waste you want rid of followed by reassembling and gluing the block back as it was. Those thin band saw cuts disappear, and once sanded smooth and finished, the block almost looks like it was never cut apart. It occurred to me that the same process could be applied to this attractive and practical napkin ring set and matching holder.

WOOD AND WORKPIECE CONSIDERATIONS

This isn't a food-contact item so any hardwood at all is OK – cherry, walnut and figured maple would all be good choices. However, we haven't used any exotics so far – as discussed in the opening chapter, exotics and food prep don't always play well together – but for utility items, they're fine. For this project, as well as the Bottle Opener project that follows, I'll be using marblewood, a remarkably beautiful wood with dark brown/black streaks running randomly through a lighter yellow/brown background. The continuous-grain appearance makes this project even more striking.

An important thing to keep in mind when making band saw boxes or other projects like this is that the main workpiece you're cutting absolutely must be well seasoned. If the wood isn't dry, you're going to

1

The first cut defines the front tilt of the entire project.

find everything warping and possibly cracking soon after cutting – sometimes as fast as within a few minutes. Dry stock is a must.

While the band saw creates a very thin kerf, it does remove material. Plus, the cutting and shaping of the individual rings removes a bit more. As a result the overall size of the completed box will be a bit smaller than what you started with. I've found that the best way to make these types of boxes is to decide on a finished size, and then add maybe ¼" all around to the size of your starting workpiece.

TAKE A WOOD BLOCK APART

I've designed this with some complimentary angles, so the first step depends on what you use to cut the outside of the workpiece. On a table saw (which is fine for the outer cuts, as the thick kerf from that tool isn't an issue), tilt the blade to 5° and cut off the face of the block. On the band saw, tilt the table 5° and cut. (**PHOTO 1**) As we switch to the interior cuts, use the band saw exclusively for the following steps.

Return the band saw table to its level position, and then slice off the

With the next cut, slice off the holder back.

A third cut removes the holder base.

A series of cuts separates the rings and end pieces.

This quick reassembly after cutting shows the relative positions of all the pieces.

¼" holder back, as in **PHOTO 2**. Be sure when you make this cut that the 90° top or bottom face of the workpiece is on the table, not the angled front. Then mark it for the part's location and orientation, and put it aside.

Reset the band saw fence to make a ⅜" cut, and cut off the holder base. (**PHOTO 3**) Again, check that the 90° back face is down on the table.

Mark the workpiece for the holder ends and the individual napkin rings per the Napkin Ring Pattern on page 102; it's a good idea to number the pieces before cutting to help keep them in order. Using a miter gauge, squarely cut off the first end piece followed by the rings and the opposite end piece, as in **PHOTO 4**. By the way, the rings are marked at 1"

intervals, but after cutting and sanding the rings should be ¹⁵⁄₁₆" as noted on the Cut List.

To illustrate what this will all look like, after cutting I did a quick reassembly of all the parts so you can see the relative positions of how everything goes back together. (**PHOTO 5**) Even without any further work you can get an idea of the continuous-grain effect.

In use, rolled napkins fit neatly into a hole in each ring, drilled with a 1½" Forstner bit. A drill press works best for this, but you can also use a hand drill. Either way, it's wise to use an easy-to-make jig that holds each piece securely while drilling to not only increase accuracy and ease of drilling, but also it's far safer. (**PHOTO 6**) You can see details about the jig in

"Safe and Steady Drill Jig" on page 103.

We'll sand all the outer surfaces later, but at this point give the ring sides a good sanding, best done on a flat surface, as in **PHOTO 7**. Don't go hog wild with the sanding here. You want to remove a minimum of material, but still get all the saw marks off and make the sides nice and smooth. Work up through the grits as needed, finishing with #220-grit. At this time, sand the inside of the holes and all the angled ring edges as well.

Also sand the bottom and back of each end piece, the inner surface of the holder back, and the top surface of the holder base to remove saw marks. These surfaces don't need finish-sanding like the sides of the rings, just a cleanup and general smoothing.

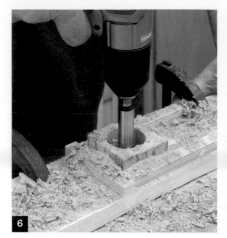

Drill a 1½" hole in the center of each ring. A holding jig makes the task easier and safer.

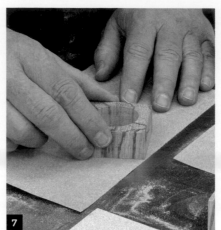

Sand the sides and holes of the rings smooth, finishing with #220-grit.

Begin the reassembly by gluing and clamping the two end pieces to the holder base.

Cut the ends of the holder at a 10° angle.

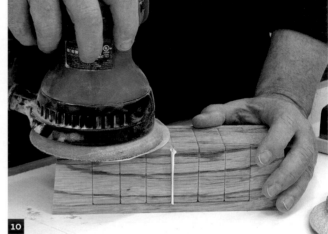

A folded piece of paper shims the rings firmly enough that the assembly can be sanded as a unit.

Arrange the rings and both ends on the holder base and mark the locations of the end pieces, allowing a bit of wiggle room for the rings. The cutting and sanding will have slightly shortened everything in between, so the ends will be inset a bit in their new locations. Glue and clamp the ends into place on your marks. (**PHOTO 8**)

When the assembly has cured, glue and clamp the holder back into place and allow the glue to completely dry.

Now, angle the ends of the holder. We're back to the outside of the assembly, so the cut can be made on table saw with the blade tilted 10°, or on the band saw with the table tilted

the same amount. (**PHOTO 9**)

Final sanding is most effective by putting the rings in place and sanding everything as a unit. With the rings lined up in the holder, slip a piece of folder paper into the center gap to shim the rings snuggly in place, then sand up through the grits to #220-grit, or maybe just a bit higher for a really smooth appearance. (**PHOTO 10**)

Marblewood is extremely hard and dense, so after sanding to a high grit you'll notice that the wood already has some sheen to it. Likewise, the dense wood doesn't need that much protection, so only minimal finishing is needed. I gave these rings

a single quick application of boiled linseed oil and only let it penetrate for a few minutes before wiping off the excess, then buffed it to a nice shine the following day.

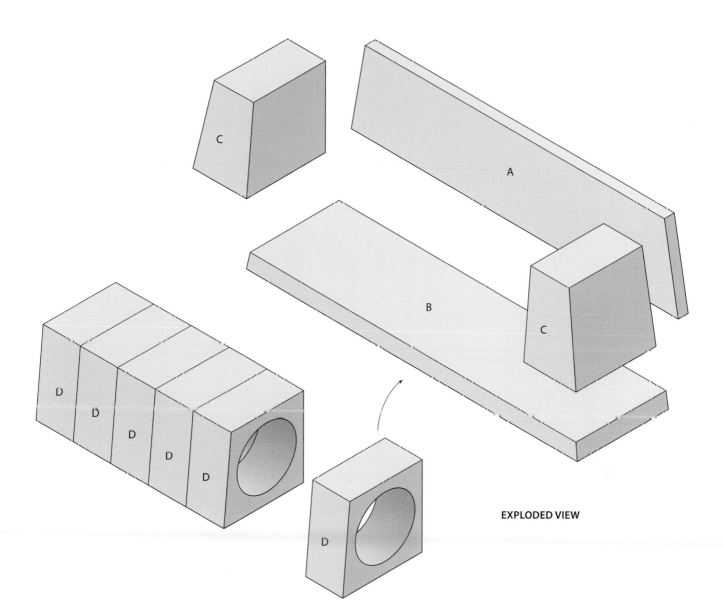

EXPLODED VIEW

NAPKIN RINGS CUT LIST

Overall Dimensions: 2⁵⁄₁₆" deep x 2³⁄₈" high x 8³⁄₈" long

REF	QTY	PART	STOCK	THICKNESS	WIDTH	LENGTH
A	1	Holder Back	Marblewood	¼"	2³⁄₈"	8³⁄₈"
B	1	Holder Base	Marblewood	³⁄₈"	2¼"	8³⁄₈"
C	2	Holder Ends	Marblewood	1¼"	2"	2"
D	6	Rings	Marblewood	¹⁵⁄₁₆"	2"	2

NOTES:

Although listed above as separate components, all parts are cut from a single block of wood.

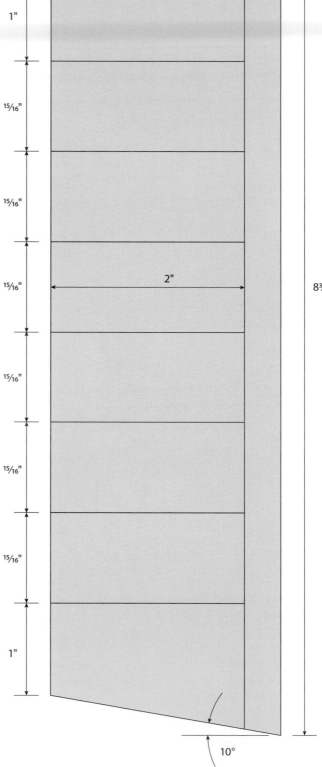

2³⁄₈"

1"

¹⁵⁄₁₆"

¹⁵⁄₁₆"

¹⁵⁄₁₆"

¹⁵⁄₁₆"

¹⁵⁄₁₆"

¹⁵⁄₁₆"

¹⁵⁄₁₆"

1"

2"

8³⁄₈"

10°

NAPKIN RING PATTERN

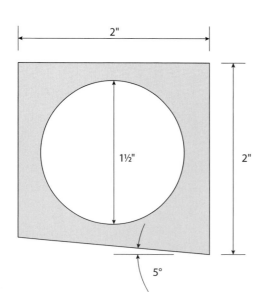

2"

1½"

2"

5°

SAFE AND STEADY DRILL JIG

Forstner bits are fabulous for drilling holes larger than ½" or so. Using Forstner bits with large workpieces is fairly straightforward by clamping the workpiece down.

But as the bit gets larger – and the workpiece smaller – controlling the workpiece becomes difficult with clamps. And you sure don't want to hold a small workpiece with your fingers using the 1½" bit you'll need for the napkin rings in this project. Not only is it extremely dangerous to have fingers that close to the bit, it's hard to even hang on to the workpiece. Instead, use this very quick-to-make drilling jig.

Select a piece of scrap wide enough for the workpiece [and some ½" x ½" or ¾" x ¾" strips] long enough so you can clamp it to a bench or drill press table. Glue and nail a strip on one side, then another at one end of that strip at a right angle. Now, place the workpiece into the angle, then glue and nail a third strip on the edge of workpiece such that it holds the workpiece nice and snug.

The jig takes only minutes to make, but it'll give you plenty of peace of mind when drilling.

ACCESSORIES

✦

ANY COOK WILL TELL YOU THE CULINARY PROCESS IS

ultimately all about the meal, but will quickly add that a lot of things

have to work together to ensure an enjoyable kitchen experience. Chief

among these are items that, while not always directly involved with

actual cooking, still play an important role in meal preparation and

presentation. ✦ The accessories presented here range from an incredibly

simple project you can hold in one hand to a major piece of household

furniture, but all make working in the kitchen easier and more

efficient – a couple even extend the kitchen experience

outside to the barbecue grill.

✦

19

Bottle Opener

IN THE LAST FEW YEARS, woodworking suppliers have introduced a host of hardware for lathe-turned items for the kitchen, and I couldn't be happier. I really enjoy the lathe, and being able to make my own kitchen and serving gear is a real treat.

In almost all cases, the hardware is threaded on one end and fits into a handle that you turn to the appropriate size. Attachment is made easy with a threaded insert epoxied into the front of the handle. And because the threaded inserts pretty much come in just two standard sizes (¼" and ⁵⁄₁₆"), you can even swap out hardware and functions like a Swiss Army knife.

The project here is a handle – it's the hardware end that does the work, and in every case it's made of metal – so there are no food-contact issues and any hardwood you want to use is fine. I enjoyed working with marblewood in the previous project and was eager to find out what it was like on the lathe, so you'll see it once again here. Good thing I bought plenty.

As to the type of utensil to make, I knew my son-in-law wanted a bottle opener to use on his deck that was too big to lose, so I thought that would be the perfect hardware here. Everything described here will be specific to the bottle opener, but the procedure would be exactly the same for any type of handle you want to make.

PREPARE THE BLANK

Cut a blank from the wood of choice. For a bottle opener, a blank 1½" square and at least 6" long is good. With the blank cut, mark the center point on each end, as in **PHOTO 1**. Once again, my little center finder comes in handy.

Drill a hole sized and to a depth specified with the hardware you plan to use. This bottle opener uses a ⁵⁄₁₆"-18 insert, so I needed to drill a ½" hole at least 1½" deep. In **PHOTO 2**, I'm using the same vertical drilling jig I used back in the Cruet Project to guarantee a perfectly vertical hole in the blank.

1 Mark the centers of the turning blank ends.

2 Drill a hole sized to accept the hardware's threaded insert.

3 Dab a small amount of epoxy into the hole, and use an Allen wrench to insert the threaded insert.

Mix up and dab just a small amount of epoxy into the hole at the end of the blank, and use an Allen wrench to drive the insert into place, as in **PHOTO 3**. Drive the insert so it's just a hair below the wood surface. You only need a very small amount of epoxy here to secure the insert, so don't go overboard or you might get it into the threads. To be sure, use a Q-tip to swab out any epoxy that may have gotten on the inside. If you don't and you mount the blank before the epoxy is cured, you may find that you can't get the blank off the mandrel. (Don't ask me how I know this.)

While the epoxy is curing, mount a chuck into your lathe's headstock, and chuck up a mandrel sized for the insert and the project. All woodworking suppliers who make kitchen

hardware also offer mandrels sized for them. The mandrel not only secures the blank to the lathe, but the width of the mandrel shoulder – 1" for the bottle opener – ensures that the top of the handle will be the exact size to mate with the hardware. When the epoxy on the blank has cured, simply twist it into place on the mandrel. (**PHOTO 4**) With the blank mounted on the mandrel, bring up the lathe tailstock and secure it against the blank on your center mark on the other end.

ONE GOOD TURN

If you're familiar with spindle turning, creating the handle is pretty straightforward. Begin at a lower speed and use a scraper or roughing gouge to turn the square blank into a

4 With the mandrel secured in a lathe chuck, twist the blank into place.

5 Rough-turn the blank into a uniform cylinder.

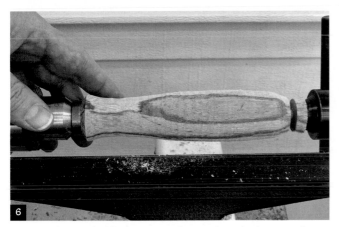

6 Continue shaping the blank, stopping frequently to check your work.

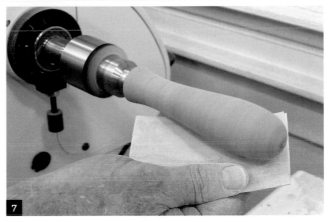

7 With the fully shaped handle spinning, sand through the grits until smooth.

uniform cylinder of the diameter of the desired handle. (**PHOTO 5**)

Switch to your preferred spindle-turning tool and kick the lathe speed up a notch or two and start shaping the handle. You can use the Bottle Opener Pattern on page 108 as a guide, or create whatever profile best fits your hand. A parting tool defines the end of the handle at the desired length. (**PHOTO 6**) Stop turning frequently to check your progress, and with the lathe fully stopped try out how the handle feels. When you have the profile just the way you want it – seriously, doing it by feel is the best way – separate the tailstock end with a parting tool or the tip of a skew.

Back off the tool rest and tailstock, and sand through the grits till you have a silky smooth surface, as in **PHOTO 7**. I like my turnings really smooth, and so sanded up to

#600-grit and then burnished the turning with a handful of shavings. It practically shined by the time I was through.

For a bit more shine, I opted to apply a coat of paste wax and, when dry, polished the handle on the lathe at high speed, as in **PHOTO 8**.

Your handle is now done and ready to be put to immediate use. Just unscrew it from the mandrel and twist in the bottle opener hardware till it seats firmly, and you're ready to head to the refrigerator and open the cold beverage of your choice.

By the way, there's a small downside to creating kitchen items with custom-turned hardwood handles: They're incredibly addictive to make.

Fortunately, as soon guests and visiting family see them, you're sure to be asked to make more.

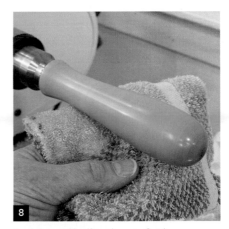

8 Applying and buffing the wax finish goes quickly on the lathe.

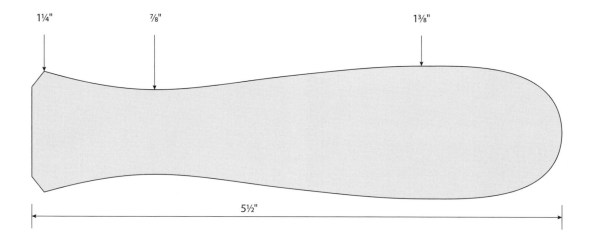

1¼"   ⅞"   1⅜"

5½"

BOTTLE OPENER PATTERN

BOTTLE OPENER CUT LIST

Overall Dimensions: 1¾" (opener width) x 1⅜" (handle width) x 8" (length)

QTY	PART	STOCK	THICKNESS	WIDTH	LENGTH
1	Opener Handle Blank	Marblewood	1½"	1½"	6" (a)

NOTES:

(a) This is the size of the turning blank; finished size of the project handle is 1⅜" x 5½"

ADDITIONAL MATERIALS:

Bottle Opener Hardware

Turning Mandrel Sized to Opener Hardware Base

Threaded Insert (⁵⁄₁₆"-18 or ¼"-20, depending on bottle-opener hardware requirement)

ONE PROCESS, MANY OPTIONS

Although I've used the lathe to make a bottle opener in this project, you can use the exact same procedure to create numerous kitchen and serving items. The overall lathe process is the same, after all – take a square piece of wood and transform it into a handle shape – but woodworking suppliers have made a variety of hardware and fittings that are often interchangeable. The bottom line is that if you can think of a kitchen item with a handle, chances are good there's a hardware kit available for it. All you need is a lathe and a piece of wood.

As with the bottle opener in this project the hardware generally screws into place, usually with a threaded insert. A mandrel used during turning ensures that the attachment point for the hardware is just the right size. Some hardware of this type has unthreaded shanks you just glue into a hole in the handle.

The photo here shows a sampling of items available from Rockler Woodworking. Clockwise from lower left: threaded inserts, $\frac{5}{16}$" and $\frac{1}{4}$" turning mandrels, 4-piece cheese knife set, coffee scoop, pie/pizza slice server, ice cream scoop, pizza cutter, bottle opener, and cheese plane.

20

Paper Towel Holder

I HAVE OAK CABINETRY, SO when adding a wooden kitchen accessory I often try to match the cabinets and other woodwork. When our old paper towel holder broke – an odd white ceramic thing with a chrome rod to hold the towel roll – making my own replacement out of oak seemed only natural.

Some towel holders, like our old one, are open on the top and the roll just slips on. I think a holder is more attractive, however, if it's designed to capture the roll at the top. With wood at the bottom, back and top, the holder presented here gives a nice wooden wrap-around appearance. The lower half is solid, but the top is articulated with a box joint that allows the top to pivot up and down to replace the towel roll as needed. In fact, the box joint here, although made with ½" joint fingers instead of ¼" fingers, is just like the corner joints of the Vintage Recipe Box presented earlier

GETTING STARTED

Begin construction by cutting the components to size. There are only three main pieces: a round base and a two-part frame consisting of a back and top. For the base, I cut an 8" x 8" square blank on the table saw from a larger piece of oak. (**PHOTO 1**) The frame back and top, meanwhile, are cut to length from standard 1x4 oak, which actually measures 3½" in width.

Since the process for creating the box joint that mates the two frame pieces is identical to what we did with the Vintage Recipe Box, I won't repeat everything in detail; just refer back to that project for the specifics. One thing to keep in mind here, though, is to create the joint right where you cut that 1x4 to create the two pieces. This will give an almost continuous grain appearance to enhance the wrap-around effect. To make the joint, set up your box joint jig as for the Recipe Box, and cut the joints in the two mating frame ends. (**PHOTO 2**)

Cut the workpieces to size on the table saw. The base blank is an 8" x 8" square.

With a box joint jig on the router table, cut the finger joints for the articulating holder frame.

3

With the frame clamped and square, drill a ¼" hole for the pivot dowel.

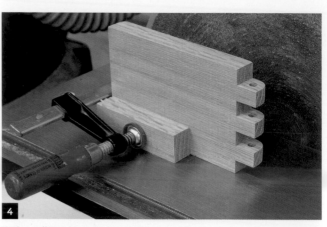

4

With small "outriggers" clamped to the workpiece to keep it square, sand the roundover on each of the frame joints.

5

Rout a 3½"-wide mortise to accommodate the frame back piece.

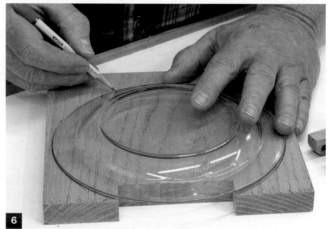

6

Use a compass or any round object – this plate was the perfect size – to draw a 7½" circle on the base.

Now, fit the joint together and clamp it securely. Check the assembly for square, and drill a ¼" hole side-to-side through the joint, as in **PHOTO 3**. This hole will accept a dowel later to create the pivoting joint.

To allow the articulated frame to function smoothly, the mating ends of the joint fingers must be rounded on the inner corners. The easiest way to do this is with a disc sander. To keep the workpieces square, clamp a short length of scrap to each side, as in **PHOTO 4**. These two pieces act as outriggers to keep the workpiece vertical.

As you round over the ends, test the articulation occasionally by slipping the pivot pin into place between the two frame pieces. Once you have

it exact, give the frame pieces a good sanding all around up to #150-grit.

A SOLID BASE

Mark an end-grain edge on the base blank in the center for a ¾" x 3½" mortise to accept the frame. You can cut this mortise with a dado set on a table saw, with a jigsaw or coping saw, or even on the band saw. However, since I already had my finger-joint jig set up, I just adjusted the bit height and cut the mortise there. (**PHOTO 5**)

To shape the base you can use a compass or any suitable round object – in **PHOTO 6**, a 7½" plate that I'd just had a sandwich on worked perfectly. (Yes, I brushed the crumbs off first.) The circle should intersect the mortise at the back corners.

Cut the base with a jigsaw or band saw. You can see in **PHOTO 7** how the edges of the circle cross the corners of the mortise.

To mark the location for the towel post, first find the center of the circle (at 7½" in diameter, the center will be 3¾" from the circle's edge). However, once you find the center, move your mark forward a bit to accommodate the inset thickness of the frame at the back and keep the roll centered in the open area. Use a 1" Forstner bit to drill a hole ½" to ⅝" deep on your mark, as in **PHOTO 8**. With the hole drilled, give the base a good sanding up to #150-grit.

ASSEMBLY AND FINISHING

To secure the pivot pin in the frame's

A band saw makes quick work of cutting out the base.

Drill a 1" hole to accept the towel post dowel.

Apply glue into the hole in the last joint finger, and slide the pivot dowel into place.

Apply glue into the base mortise, then drive screws into countersunk holes to secure the frame back to the base.

articulated joint, slip a slightly over-length ¼" dowel into place, stopping just before it enters the last joint finger on the side. Dab a bit of glue into the hole on that side, and a bit on the dowel shaft on the other side just before it enters the frame. (**PHOTO 9**) Tapping the dowel home draws glue into the outer hole on one side, while it slides into the glue on the other. (This is the same way we secured the pivot dowel in the Spring Tongs project earlier.) You'll definitely have glue squeeze-out on both sides, so

wipe it off quickly with a damp rag. When the glue has dried, trim the dowel flush and sand smooth.

Clamp the base to your bench or worktable, drill a pair of countersunk holes into the frame and base. Apply a bit of glue into the mortise, and secure the frame to the base with 1½" screws. (**PHOTO 10**)

To complete the holder, thoroughly sand the towel post and glue it into the hole drilled in the base. Then give the entire assembly a few coats of the finish of your choice. I opted to leave

the oak plain and give it a finish of satin polyurethane. However, if your cabinetry is darker – or you simply want a darker towel holder – stain the assembly before finishing.

This holder accommodates regular- and large-sized rolls of paper towels perfectly. However, now that jumbo-sized rolls of towels are available you may wish to make your holder a bit larger. If so, you'll only need to change the size of the base and the location of the towel post.

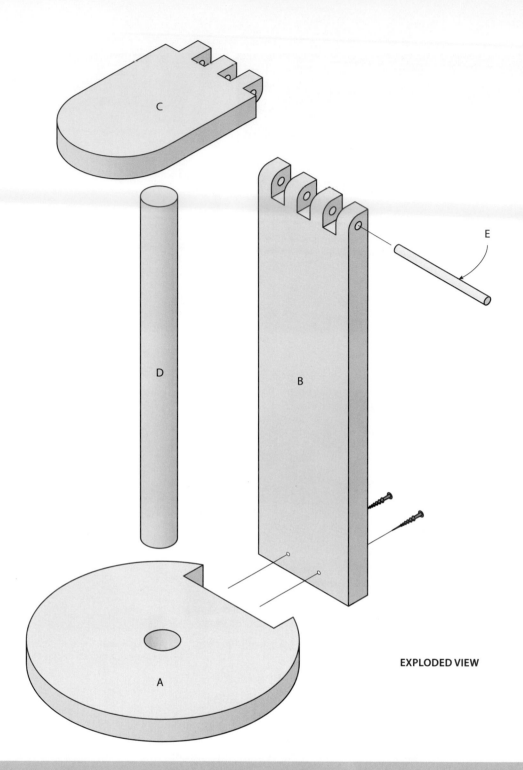

EXPLODED VIEW

PAPER TOWEL HOLDER CUT LIST

Overall Dimensions: 7½" x 7½" x 13"

REF	QTY	PART	STOCK	THICKNESS	WIDTH	LENGTH
A	1	Base Blank	Oak	¾"	8"	8"
B	1	Frame Back	Oak	¾"	3½"	13" (a)
C	1	Frame Top	Oak	¾"	3½"	6" (a)
D	1	Towel Post	Oak Dowel	1"	n/a	11½"
E	1	Pivot Pin	Hardwood Dowel	¼"	n/a	3½"

NOTES:

(a) Can be cut from standard 1x4 oak, which actually measures ¾" thick by 3½" wide.

Kitchen Island

WOODWORKERS OFTEN SAY "You can never have enough clamps." Of course, that truism is specific to a woodshop. In my other workshop – the kitchen – there's a similar truism: "You can never have enough counter space."

No matter how big or small the kitchen, counter space to get work done is always at a premium. It's not possible to add more countertops without a major kitchen redesign, but if you have a bit of floor space you can add more worksurface with a kitchen island like the one presented here. As a bonus, you automatically get more storage, and because this isn't a permanent structure you can move it around as needed.

DESIGN CONSIDERATIONS
A kitchen island's size and design are limited only by the available room and cabinet arrangement. My kitchen isn't large, so at 24" x 36" this one fits our needs perfectly, and at 36" high it matches our existing countertops. Adjust the overall size and height to suit your kitchen and work habits.

You can configure the openings underneath the worktop any way you like. I'll talk about some of the options to consider later, but for this one I've incorporated a wine rack into the open end. Meanwhile, the open front section accommodates – at my wife's request – decorative wicker baskets separated by an adjustable shelf.

Unlike the projects so far, this one's a piece of furniture. As such, your material choices are wide open. If you plan to cut and prep food directly on the top, use only a closed-grain hardwood. Otherwise, any other wood species is fine, but hardwood is still best for the top.

I've elected to use ambrosia maple for the top and the visible portions of the wine rack and basket shelves. For the frame and most of the internal components I went with select pine, which is strong and blemish-free, as well as lighter than hardwood. The shelves are high-quality Baltic birch plywood, while the base is a strong,

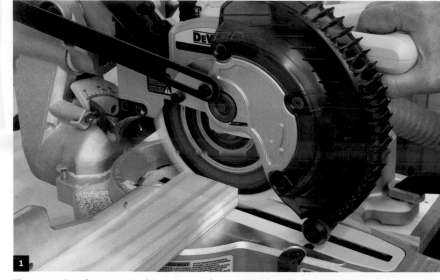

1 There are a lot of crosscuts in this project, and a miter saw handles the task quickly and accurately.

heavy piece of MDF. Finally, for the paneling I opted for beadboard wainscoting, one of my favorite looks for the kitchen. You can buy beadboard several ways – solid wood, routed plywood, hardboard sheets, etc. – but I found that fiberboard wainscoting was a good choice as there are no seasonal movement issues like with wood, it's heavier and more substantial than big sheets (some of which are downright floppy), and they're a full ¼" thick. The 32"-long pieces measure about 7" in width, and are tongue-and-grooved so it's easy to glue them up to whatever size panel you want. Best of all, they're already primed and ready for painting.

By the way, this will be a heavy piece of furniture and we'll need to flip it every which way during construction. For that reason, we'll save permanently attaching a number of things – especially the base and top – till the end to keep the weight down as long as possible. As you work, you may want to enlist a helper to assist moving the cabinet around at key points.

START WITH THE FRAMES
The kitchen island's main carcase is basic frame-and-panel cabinet construction, so the first order of busi-

2 Prepare the frame components by drilling pocket holes in the inner surfaces of the rail ends. Note the line I've marked on the stock that indicates where the rabbet will go.

ness is to cut a bunch of stock to size for the panel stiles and rails – 17 in all. (**PHOTO 1**) Although based on standard 1x3 lumber, I wanted both sides of the mating corners to be the same size. To achieve that, each mating corner consists of a wide stile that's off-the-rack 1x3 measuring 2½" wide. For the narrow sides of the corners, just rip four 1x3s to 1¾". Hang on to the offcuts from those rip cuts; we'll use them later.

I love pocket-hole joinery for panel frames, as it's fast, easy and very strong. Drill a pair of pocket

Assemble the frames with 1¼" pocket screws.

Rout a ½"-wide rabbet around the inner edge of each frame receiving a beadboard panel. Measure your exact panel thickness, and set the depth of the rabbet accordingly.

Cut the panels to size.

Round the corners of each panel and secure them into the rabbets with ¼" narrow-crown staples.

holes in the inside ends of each of the rails and the center stile, as in **PHOTO 2**. Keep in mind when locating the holes that there will be a ½"-wide rabbet on one edge, so it's a good idea to mark the stock to avoid drilling a pocket hole in this area.

Assemble each of the frames with pocket screws. I make a lot of frames, and in **PHOTO 3** you can see my assembly jig. This is just a sheet of ½" plywood to which I've attached strips at an exact right angle. I just nestle the stile/rail combo into the corner, clamp it down and drive the screws.

Three of the panels are simple frames, but the front panel has a dividing center stile located to create a 14" opening on the right for the baskets per the Front Panel Layout drawing on page 124.

Install a ½" rabbeting bit in your router table or handheld router, and cut the rabbet on the inside edge of each section of frame that receives a panel. (**PHOTO 4**) My beadboard is exactly ¼" thick so that's the depth I've set, but measure your beadboard and adjust the depth accordingly. Remember that the frame at the wine rack end of the island, as well as the portion of the frame around the basket opening on the front right have no panels, so no rabbets there.

Cut your beadboard panels to width, as in **PHOTO 5**. Before installing the panels you can use a chisel to square those rabbet corners, but I

found it easier and faster to simply round off the panel corners with a jigsaw to fit. Apply a bead of glue all around the rabbets and drop the beadboard into place, then secure with ½" narrow-crown staples, as in **PHOTO 6**. By the way, a benefit of using fiberboard panels is that the staples will seat just below the surface; once lightly sanded the staples are nearly invisible.

CARCASE ASSEMBLY

With the framed panels complete, you've essentially made the four sides of a box – let's build that box.

Apply glue to the mating edges of the panels with the narrow stiles (the front and back), making sure that

7

Glue and clamp the carcase together. A brad nailer adds strength, and keeps the frame corners flush while clamping.

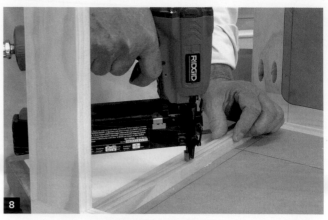

8

Attach the end shelf support with glue and brads first, followed by the front and back shelf supports

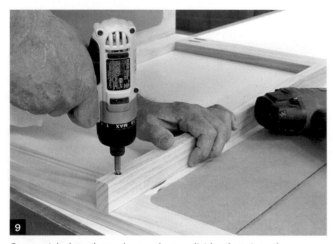

9

Countersink, then glue and screw the two divider cleats into place on opposite sides of the carcase.

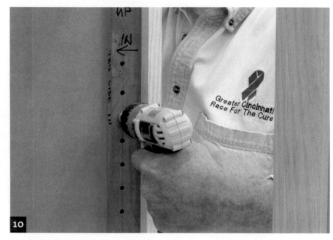

10

A drill guide like this one made from a hardwood scrap accurately sets the shelf pin holes and helps to keep the drill at 90° as you work.

they go inside the wide-stile panels on each end. Then, on a level worksurface, lightly clamp the carcase at the corners just tightly enough to keep the box shape. Adjust the corners flush, and drive in a 1½" to 2" brad. The brads hold everything in perfect alignment while you fully clamp up the rest of the assembly. (**PHOTO 7**) I found that four or five brads at each corner hold everything aligned just right as you work the clamps.

When the assembly has dried, flip it onto the basket end to begin attaching the shelf supports. These supports, by the way, are cut to length from the ⅝" x ¾" offcuts from when we ripped the narrow stiles to width. They should be located so the top edge is ½" below the basket opening

to allow the lower shelf to fit into place flush with the front rail. Attach the end shelf support first with glue and brads, as in **PHOTO 8**. Flip the carcase as needed to give access to attach the front and back shelf supports in the same manner.

A sheet of ¼" Baltic birch plywood forms the divider between the two sections, and is mounted to a pair of 1x2 pine cleats. With the carcase on its side, apply glue to one edge of the cleat and countersink and screw it to the frame so it butts up against the front/back shelf supports, as in **PHOTO 9**, then repeat on the other side. The divider and cleats aren't structural to the carcase, so glue and a single screw on each end will do the trick. With the cleats installed, attach

the divider shelf support.

Let's drill the shelf-pin holes before installing the divider since reaching inside is easier now. Create a shelf-pin guide by drilling a series of holes sized to the shelf pin shafts 1" from the edge of a piece of hardwood scrap long enough to register with the bottom of the cabinet. Standard hole spacing is 32mm, or about 1¼", and it's best to drill the holes in the guide with a drill press to ensure 90° holes. Drill the first hole so it falls where it will keep the middle shelf centered in the basket opening, then add as many holes on either side of it as you want. Now, place the guide into each corner of the basket opening, and drill the holes in the sides to the depth specified for your shelf

Cut the divider to size, then attach to the divider cleats with glue and brads.

Notch the corners of the bottom shelf to fit around the two divider cleats. Use the hole in the back to lift the shelf to access the hidden compartment.

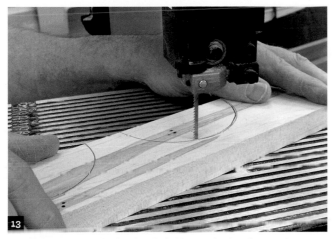

Cut all the curves on the four bottle holders with a band saw, as here, or with a jigsaw.

Secure the mounting cleats to the backs of the bottle holders with glue and countersunk screws.

pins. Note in **PHOTO 10** that I've clearly marked my drilling guide for correct orientation, and that I've attached a depth stop to the drill bit.

Now, cut the plywood divider to size, and attach it to the wine rack side of the cleats with glue and brads. (**PHOTO 11**)

Cut the two shelves to size, with notches on the left-hand corners to fit around the divider cleats as in **PHOTO 12**. The bottom shelf is cut to fit snuggly down into the opening, but the middle shelf should be ¾" shorter to accommodate the hardwood trim on the front. For that trim I cut a ¾" x 1" piece of the same ambrosia maple used for the top, and glued and clamped it to the front of the middle shelf.

Oh, you may be wondering why there's a hole in the back of the lower shelf in **PHOTO 12**. That's a secret – a secret compartment, that is. The lower shelf isn't attached, but just drops into place. Drill a 1" hole in the back to act as a finger hole to lift the shelf out to access the space underneath. With the basket in place, no one will ever know it's there.

Remove both shelves for now, as we'll be flipping the carcase around a couple more times. Fill the tiny nail holes from the brads, and give the carcase a good sanding inside and out up to #150-grit.

WINE RACK

Use the Bottle Holder Pattern on page 124 to mark the eight bottle

holder workpieces, then cut out the curved portions the bottles rest in. I'm using a band saw in **PHOTO 13**, but you could use a jigsaw. For the front holders, which are visible, I used more of that beautiful ambrosia maple; for the back holder and all the mounting cleats I used select pine.

Attach the holder mounting cleats to the backs of the holders at the edges with glue and countersunk screws. (**PHOTO 14**) For the back rack, the bottom edge of the bottle holders should be at 2", 8⅜", 14¾" and 21⅛" from the bottom of the cleat. For the front rack, raise each of the holders by ⅜". This will level the bottles a bit. They'll still cant downward at the cork, but won't be quite so prone to sliding forward when stored in the rack.

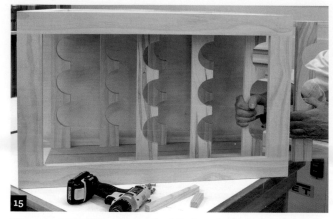

Slip each wine rack into place to check for fit and adjust as needed. We'll attach them permanently a bit later.

A biscuit joiner makes fast work of cutting the slots for the tabletop fastener hardware.

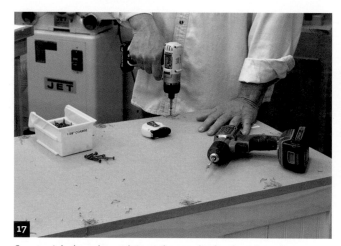

Countersink, then glue and screw the two divider cleats into place on opposite sides of the carcase.

Install the four feet to the underside of the carcase base.

Sand the racks up to #150-grit, then do a test fit of each by slipping them in through the top of the carcase, and adjust the fit if necessary. (**PHOTO 15**) The faces of the front bottle holders should be 3" from the outside of the frame opening. The back rack's holder faces should be 10½" from the outside of the opening. With the racks set, temporarily clamp them into place.

FROM BOTTOM TO TOP

Flip the carcase vertical to cut the slots for the tabletop fasteners. These slots engage a series of clip-like fasteners screwed to the underside of the kitchen island worktop to hold it tightly in place, yet still allow for seasonal expansion and contraction. The

tabletop fasteners you get will specify the slot depth, and distance from the top edge. A biscuit joiner is the perfect tool for cutting these slots, as in **PHOTO 16**, but you could also cut them with a router fitted with a slot-cutting bit. As you cut, avoid the pocket screws and wine-rack mounting cleats, although you may need to unclamp the front rack temporarily to get the slot up the cleat edge. Two slots on each end, and three on each side is good.

With the slots cut, now's a good time to consider internal finishing; it'll be harder once the top and bottom are attached. Slide out the racks and paint/varnish them according to your preferences, and then also finish the inside walls of the wine and

basket sections as desired. The two shelve are not permanently attached, so they can be finished anytime.

Attach the two wine racks by driving countersunk screws into the top and bottom of each mounting cleat and into the carcase frame.

Flip the carcase over and put the base into place. Countersink and drive an even dozen 1⅝" screws around the perimeter to secure the base. (**PHOTO 17**)

Now, mark locations for the feet – the exact location of the mounting hole is determined by the foot diameter, but insetting the feet about ¼" on each edge is good – then drill on your marks. (**PHOTO 18**) For the feet I got, the holes were located 1¾" in. These standard furniture feet are

Glue up the panel for the kitchen island top, then clamp together till dry.

Drill pilot holes for each of the tabletop fasteners, and attach with the screws provided with the hardware.

available from any home center but their dimensions will vary, so measure before drilling and adjust accordingly. Most will take either a ¼" or ⁵⁄₁₆" hole, and will screw securely into the hole itself. If you prefer, you could drill larger holes for threaded inserts, but that's not really necessary.

Glue up the worktop from the hardwood of your choice. (**PHOTO 19**) When dry, sand and level both sides up to #150-grit.

With the worktop upside down, upend the finished cabinet atop it and center it – the 24" x 36" worktop should give you 2" overhang all around. Insert the hardware fasteners into the slots, then mark and drill pilot holes before driving in the screws to secure the worktop. (**PHOTO 20**)

Finally, cut and add some molding trim around the bottom. You can use any type of molding you like, but it should be at least an inch or so wide so it covers the transition from the wood framed panels and the MDF base at the bottom.

FINISHING THOUGHTS

As you can see in the opening photograph, I've painted all external surfaces of the carcase, using a semigloss latex enamel in a color complimenting our kitchen. For this reason, I had no hesitation in mixing and matching the materials. If you prefer natural wood or stain, then you'll need to match the species depending on the appearance you're going for.

I gave the worktop, the inside of the two open sections, the shelves and the wine racks a finish of satin polyurethane. A lot of strong protection, and the clear finish lets everyone see the beauty of that ambrosia maple.

This is an extremely customizable project. First, of course, you can alter the size as needed to better fit your working space. I sized this one to match our countertops, but if you're particularly tall or short, consider making your kitchen island an inch or two higher or lower for easier use.

Relocate the open sections any way you like – the ones here are

oriented to match work patterns in our kitchen, but you may like them a different way. Likewise, you can use those two sections any number of ways. Instead of baskets, for example, a row of drawers might suit your purposes better. Or take out the baskets and install a door to use that section as a standard cabinet. Same thing goes for the wine rack section on the end.

If your kitchen space is sufficient, you might consider widening the top on one side to allow a stool or two to fit underneath. The stool in the next chapter would be a perfect fit.

The kitchen island here is light enough to move around if needed, but it's intended to pretty much stay put. However, you can increase the versatility of yours by replacing the feet with wheels that allow it to be rolled wherever you want it, or even just rolled out of the way if you ever need to.

KITCHEN ISLAND CUT LIST

Overall Dimensions: 24" wide x 36" long x 36" high

REF	QTY	PART	STOCK	THICKNESS	WIDTH	LENGTH
A	4	Wide Frame Stiles	Pine	¾"	2½"	30" (a)
B	4	Narrow Frame Stiles	Pine	¾"	1¾"	30" (b)
C	4	End Rails	Pine	¾"	2½"	15" (a)
D	4	Front/Back Rails	Pine	¾"	2½"	27" (a)
E	1	Center Stile	Pine	¾"	2½"	25" (a)
F	1	Front Panel	Beadboard	¼"	11½"	26"
G	1	Back Panel	Beadboard	¼"	26"	28"
H	1	End Panel	Beadboard	¼"	16"	26"
I	1	End Shelf Support	Pine	¾"	⅝"	18½
J	2	Front/Back Shelf Support	Pine	¾"	⅝"	16½"
K	2	Divider Cleats	Pine	¾"	1½"	30" (c)
L	1	Divider	Baltic Birch Ply	¼"	18½"	30"
M	1	Divider Shelf Support	Pine	¾"	⅝"	17¼"
N	1	Lower Shelf	Baltic Birch Ply	½"	17¼"	18½"
O	1	Middle Shelf	Baltic Birch Ply	¾"	17¼"	17¾"
P	1	Middle Shelf Front Trim	Maple	¾"	1"	16½"
Q	8	Wine Bottle Holders	Maple/Pine	¾"	2½"	18½" (a)
R	4	Bottle Holder Cleats	Pine	¾"	1"	30"
S	1	Base	MDF or Ply	¾"	20"	32"
T	4	Feet	Poplar	n/a	n/a"	4"
U	1	Worktop	Maple	¾"	24"	36"
V	2	End Base Trim	Any	⅜"	1¼"	Cut to fit
W	2	Front/Back Base Trim	Any	⅜"	1¼"	Cut to fit

NOTES:

(a) Can be cut to length from standard 1x3 lumber, which actually measures ¾" thick by 2½" wide.

(b) Ripped to width and length from standard 1x3 lumber.

(c) Can be cut to length from standard 1x2 lumber, which actually measures ¾" thick by 1½" wide.

ADDITIONAL MATERIALS:

Shelf Pins (4 needed)

Hardwood Furniture Feet (4 needed), approximately 4" high

Tabletop Fasteners (10 needed)

Baskets (2 needed)

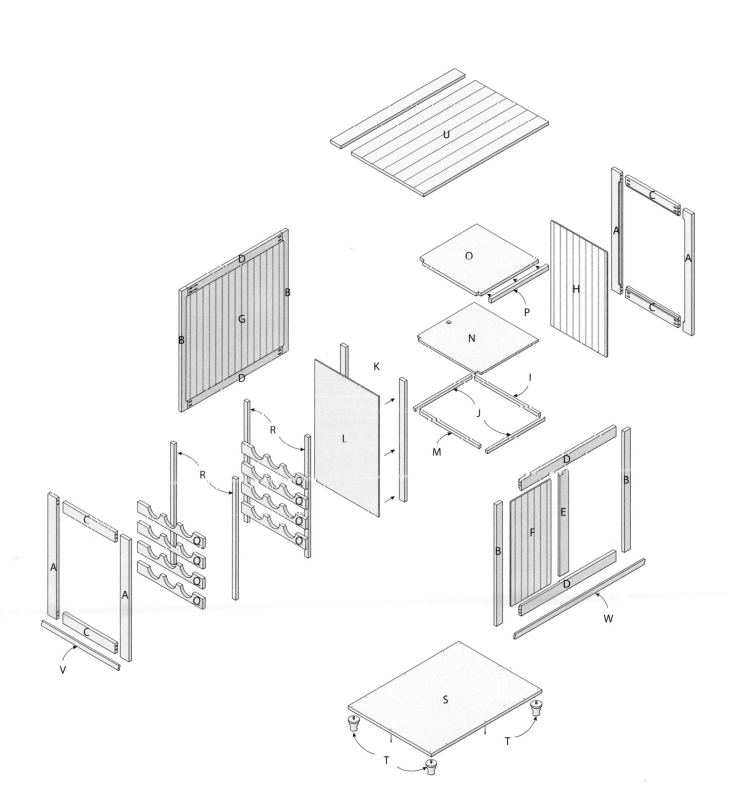

EXPLODED VIEW

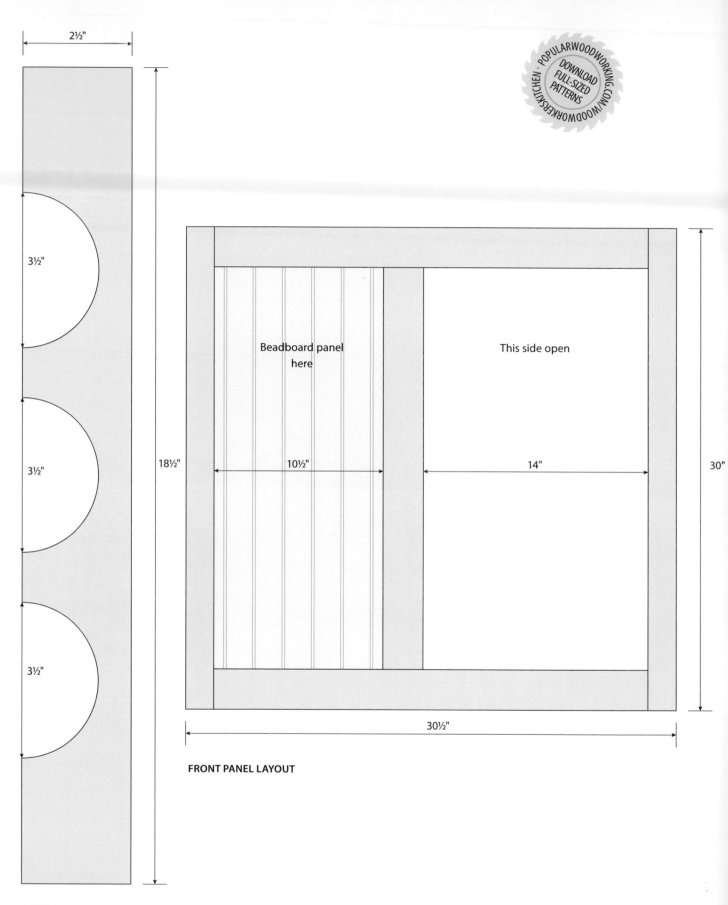

2½"

3½"

3½"

3½"

18½"

BOTTLE HOLDER PATTERN

Beadboard panel here

This side open

10½"

14"

30"

30½"

FRONT PANEL LAYOUT

Kitchen Stool

I'VE MADE LOTS OF STOOLS over the years, but for some reason never made one for our own kitchen. For one thing, our kitchen isn't that large and I just never thought we should sacrifice space for something we never thought we needed. I was introduced to the error in my thinking when I finished this stool: My wife absolutely loved it, wondering aloud (several times now) why we never had one. Naturally, I took the diplomatic way out and said I've been saving it for a surprise. Not sure she bought that, though.

Seating, especially seating that involves opposing angles, can be daunting. It's true that there are some angles here and you absolutely have to keep careful track of components so they're assembled in the correct order and direction, but there's really nothing all that complicated. And because most of the parts are available right off the rack at your local home center, much of the construction involves merely cutting things to length. With that in mind, if you've never made a stool before, this is an excellent first project to develop your skills.

1

A digital angle gauge ensures you're setting up your bevel cuts exactly right.

2

Cut the 5° angles on one end of the legs, then flip them over and repeat on the other.

3

With the legs clamped, mark the rung locations simultaneously to guarantee that they're all the same.

PREPARATION
With the exception of the seat, everything you need already comes in the right width. Start with the legs, which are nominal 2x2 oak. I say nominal because that's how they're sold, but as standard dimensional lumber it will actually measure 1½" x 1½". You'll find these at your local home center in 36" lengths. You'll need four, but grab an extra or two just to have on hand as a backup in case of an error in measuring or layout.

You could cut your own legs from a wider piece of 1½" oak, of course, but I still recommend going with these 2x2s for a good reason. Cutting thinner strips from a wider piece often releases stresses from within the wood that cause the smaller pieces to quickly warp or bend in unexpected ways. That can be disastrous

when constructing seating. However, these 2x2s have been in the rack a while and any warping they're likely to do has already occurred. Just pick through the rack and take only the straightest ones.

Same thing for the ¾" oak dowels you'll need for the rungs. Don't just buy the first ones you grab, but sight down each one and verify that it's straight. (Spoiler alert – most of them won't be.) You'll be glad you did when it comes time to assembly the stool.

As for the seat, you can either create one through lamination as we'll do here, or you can use a solid slab. I opted for walnut to compliment the oak leg set, with highlighting oak strips in the seat to tie everything together. If you prefer, though, an all-

oak stool will still be quite handsome.

Determine your stool height based on where you'll use it. As a general rule of thumb, stools work best topping out about 10" below the surface they're used with. Kitchen counters typically measure 34"-39" high, so a stool of 24"-29" work wells. Bars are higher, usually 40"-46", so size a bar stool accordingly.

The final part of preparation is really the first step of construction, and that's assuring that the 5° angles you cut are spot-on. (**PHOTO 1**) I never use the built-in gauges on tools anymore, as they can be untrustworthy and, frankly, just too difficult to read. Instead, I rely on a digital angle gauge for any beveled cut I make. If you haven't invested in one, I highly recommend them.

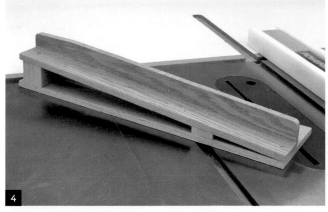

My drilling jig is a simple platform with a 5-degree tilt.

Carefully following your guides, drill the rung holes.

With the rung holes drilled, give each leg a round over on all four edges.

A crosshatch cut into the dowel ends creates more gluing surface.

MAKE THE LEG SET

With your table saw blade tilted 5° (an actual reading of 85°), cut the angles on the legs. In **PHOTO 2**, you can see that once again I've ganged my parts together to make the cuts simultaneously. Cut the foot ends of the legs, then flip the four legs over end-for-end and cut the seat ends.

Now comes literally the most important part of this project, marking the parts. Some of the trepidation for making seating with multiple angles, I believe, is getting everything going the right direction. Clearly mark the legs for direction – front/back, left/right and top/bottom.

Following your marks, clamp the legs together and mark for the rungs, as in **PHOTO 3**. Use a square to pencil a line straight across, then mark the center of the line on each leg for drilling the holes. I've offset the rungs by 1½" so they don't intersect when drilling the holes, so the rungs on the front/back of the stool are higher than those on the sides.

Drilling repeated holes at identical angles is tricky, but can be done a couple ways. If your drill press has a tilting table, you can simply angle it 5° and drill the holes. If you go this route I'd recommend clamping some sort of fence or backstop to the table to keep the leg workpiece centered so the drill bit hits the mark every time.

Or you could build a simple jig like the one in **PHOTO 4**. This is nothing more than a wooden base, to which I've attached a vertical fence. To the fence, I've attached a 2"-wide strip of wood angled at 5°. Without altering the drill press table (which can be a pain) this jig allows you to make angled holes anytime you want just by clamping it to your drill press table. I'll use this jig for years to come.

In **PHOTO 5**, you can see how I'm putting this to work. There are 16 holes to drill 1" deep for the eight rungs, so take your time with this and double check all your markings to be sure you have each leg in the correct orientation before drilling. It's very easy to make a mistake – don't ask me how I know this – so this is where those extra 2x2s I mentioned earlier come in.

Let's ease those sharp corners on the legs. Set up a roundover bit in your router table and run each leg through on all sides. (**PHOTO 6**) Now, give the legs a good sanding up to #150-grit on all four surfaces.

Cut your rungs to size per the

Apply glue into the holes and use a mallet to tap them into place.

It helps to do the final assembly and clamping on a reliably flat surface such as the top of a table saw.

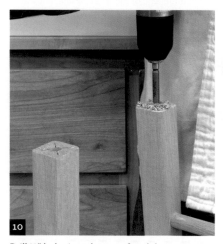

Drill ½" holes into the top of each leg to accept the dowel tenons.

Apply glue to all the seat components except in the center, and clamp up till dry.

Cut List on page 130. Rather than just glue the rungs into place with squared ends, I like to prep them a bit for a stronger, cleaner joint. (**PHOTO 7**) First, I spin the ends lightly on a disc sander to round the edges a bit. This makes assembly a bit easier and helps to distribute glue more evenly as the rung is driven home. Then, I cut a shallow crosshatch on the ends. This increases the gluing surface area for a stronger joint, and also gives excess glue someplace to go as the rung is inserted, minimizing squeeze-out.

Lay out everything in the order of assembly – first leg, second leg, etc. – and apply glue into the holes. (**PHOTO 8**) Insert each dowel in turn, seating it fully with a mallet, and remove any squeeze out that you get.

With the leg set assembled, move it to a reliably flat surface – your saw's table is a perfect choice – and clamp it up. (**PHOTO 9**)

When the leg set has dried, center and drill ½" holes 1" deep into the tops of all four legs for the dowel tenons that will join the legs to the seat. (**PHOTO 10**) My drill has a bubble level on the end that helps me to keep the holes vertical, but if you have a floor-standing drill press you can do the holes there.

TAKE A SEAT

The seat can be solid or laminated from smaller pieces of differing species as I've done here. However, although my band saw has a height capacity of 12", I still find it easier to

cut the curves with the seat halved, then join them after cutting.

When doing the seat lamination, apply glue to all the surfaces except one in the middle, then clamp up the seat. (**PHOTO 11**)

When dry, outline the seat curve on each half of the seat, then cut the curve on the band saw, as in **PHOTO 12**. With both seat halves curved, apply glue to the mating surfaces and glue up the completed seat. When dry, sand the seat all around up to #150-grit.

Place the seat upside down on your work surface and upend the leg set atop it, center it and mark the leg locations. Slip dowel centers into the holes on the legs and upend it once more onto the seat on your marks.

Cut the upper curves on the seat halves on the band saw, then glue the two halves together to complete the seat.

Transfer the tenon locations from the stool legs to the underside of the seat and drill matching ½" holes.

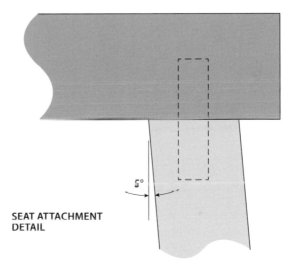

Glue the dowel tenons into the leg tops, then mate the leg set to the seat to complete the stool.

SEAT ATTACHMENT DETAIL

5°

Tap the ends of the legs with a mallet to mark the matching hole locations, and drill ½" holes 1" deep on your marks. (**PHOTO 13**)

Cut four 2" tenons from a ½" hardwood dowel, and prep the ends as we did with the rungs earlier. Apply glue into the holes on the tops of the legs and tap in the tenons with a mallet to seat them firmly. (**PHOTO 14**)

Finally, dab glue into the holes on the underside of the seat and set the leg set into place, tapping it home with the mallet. Apply clamps to the seat and top rungs to hold the seat firmly in place till dry.

We've already sanded parts individually, but a final light sanding is still a good idea before finishing. As to a coating choice, it's up to you. Once again, I've chosen polyurethane for the highest protection. I've not stained the wood, but feel free to do so on yours.

CUSTOMIZING

There are any number of changes you can make to your stool project. Stick with strong hardwood, but any species is fine. Alter the size as you like, as well as the style of the seat. This stool has squared legs, but you could also make it with round legs by using 1½" oak dowels instead of the oak 2x2s used here.

I've done this stool with legs splayed in only one direction, front-

to-back. However, by cutting compound 5° angles on the leg tops and bottoms you can splay the legs in both directions.

You can also make the stool with perfectly vertical legs. If so, I'd recommend changing the seat from rectangular to square to enlarge the footprint. The project stool's footprint is 12¼" x 13" owing to the splayed legs, making it very stable even though the seat measures 10" x 15". Straight legs will have a footprint that mirrors the seat, so widening the seat front-to-back would do the trick.

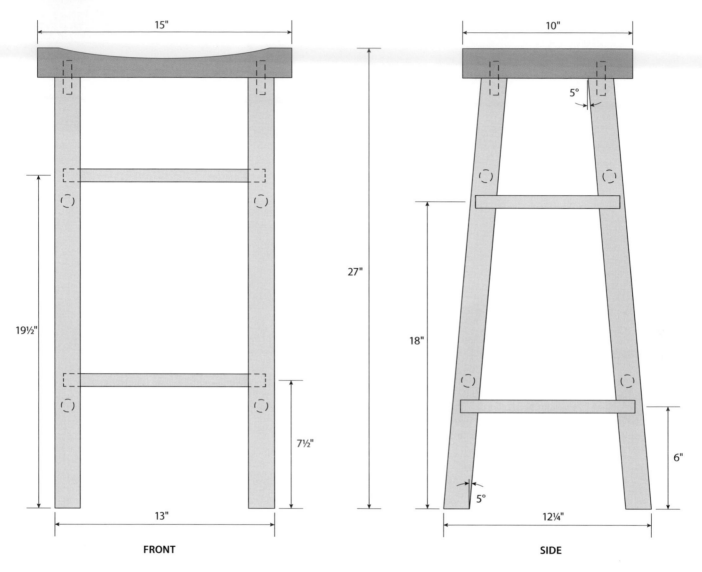

FRONT

SIDE

KITCHEN STOOL CUT LIST

Overall Dimensions: 12¼" deep x 15" wide x 27" tall

REF	QTY	PART	STOCK	THICK	WIDTH	LENGTH
A	4	Legs	Oak	1½"	1½"	25½"
B	2	Side Upper Rungs	Oak Dowel	¾"	n/a	8½"
C	2	Side Lower Rungs	Oak Dowel	¾"	n/a	10¼"
D	4	Front/Back Rungs	Oak Dowel	¾"	n/a	12"
E	1	Seat	Walnut/Oak	1¾"	10"	15"
F	4	Dowel Tenons	Harwood Dowel	½"	n/a	2"

NOTES:

Seat for the project stool is glued up of walnut and oak, but any hardwood – laminated or solid – may be used.

Grill Cart

TILL NOW, ALL OF THE KITCHEN projects we've presented are for use primarily in, well, the kitchen. But that's not the only place many of us do our best cooking. With that in mind, I thought I'd make the final two projects for my second favorite place to cook and enjoy food: outdoors.

When it comes to making outdoor projects, I'm a huge fan of Western red cedar. Not only is it an iconic look for patio and deck furniture, it stands up to the elements incredibly well. Soft, lightweight and very easy to work, cedar is perfect for outdoor projects. As a bonus, your workshop smells wonderful the entire time you're working with it.

I've sized this grill cart to my own needs, so feel free to alter dimensions for a larger or smaller cart. My grill has shelves on both sides at a more-or-less standard height of 34", so I wanted something a bit lower. It's still high enough to work with easily, but it fits perfectly underneath those shelves when not in use.

WORKING WITH CEDAR

It's important to know that cedar can be sized oddly. You buy it the same way you buy pine, oak, poplar or any other dimensional lumber – 1x3, 2x4, etc. – and like all dimensional lumber it's narrower than the nominal designation. A 1x3 is always going to actually be 2½" wide no matter what wood species it is. However, where most 1-by dimensional lumber is reliably ¾" thick (1½" thick for 2-by lumber), cedar is typically a bit thicker because it has one face that's not planed smooth, which increases the thickness a bit, usually by ⅛".

A 1x3 piece of cedar, then, can actually be around ⅞" thick. Cedar 2x4s, meanwhile, often come with all four faces rough, adding that ⅛" on all four sides. The cedar 2x4 I used for this project actually measured 1¾" x 3¾". But the amount of thickness added by the rough faces can vary, so always measure cedar before cutting project parts, and take any

Since part dimensions match off-the-shelf lumber, you'll only need to cut most of the components to length.

Assemble the legs by gluing the two sides together at a right angle.

extra thickness into account and adjust dimensions from the project cut list accordingly.

Cedar can split easily, so it's imperative to drill pilot holes before driving screws. Because of the softness – and that rough unplaned face – it's also quite splintery so handle it with care.

START WITH THE FRAME

The grill cart frame is very simple: four L-shaped legs made by gluing 1x2s and 1x3s at a right angle, and eight stretchers that tie everything together. Begin by cutting the leg and stretcher components to length. (**PHOTO 1**) Because we're using the lumber as it comes from the rack, you only need to cut the parts to length per the Cut List on page 137.

Apply glue to one edge of each 1x2, and clamp to the face of each 1x3 until dry, as in **PHOTO 2**. The resulting legs will measure 2½" in one direction, and 2¼" in the other, and in the finished cart the wider sides will face front/back, while the narrow

Starting with the ends, attach the upper and lower stretchers to create the two leg sets.

Connect the two leg sets with front/back upper and lower stretchers.

Mark the corners of the two outer shelf slats, and then cut the notches to allow the slats to nestle into the angled legs.

Install the two outer shelf slats first with glue and screws.

sides face toward the ends.

Assemble the frame by first creating the end leg sets. Lay a pair of legs on your work surface with the narrow sides downward, then drill, glue and screw the upper and lower end stretchers into place, as in **PHOTO 3**. Use two 1¼" exterior-grade screws on the end of each stretcher, and be sure to drill pilot holes first to avoid splitting the soft wood.

Now, complete the frame by attaching the upper and lower front/back stretchers into place. There's not a lot of room to work here, and in **PHOTO 4** you can see than I'm angling the pilot holes for the screws.

SHELF AND TABLETOP

Cut the four shelves to length from cedar 1x4s to make the shelf slats.

The two center slats require no preparation, but the two outer ones need to be cut to fit around the legs. Using the Notch Pattern on page 137 as a guide, mark the ends for cutting, as in **PHOTO 5**. Remember that the L-shaped pattern is shorter in one direction, so be sure to place them correctly so the short end of the pattern is on the end of the slat. With the notch marked, cut it out with a band saw, jigsaw or handsaw.

Run a bead of waterproof glue along the top of the lower front/back stretchers, then clamp the outer slats into place. Countersink and then drive a 1½" screw through the end stretcher and into each end of the outer slats, as in **PHOTO 6**. Now, add a single screw in the center of the front/back stretchers to complete

the attachment. Since this is a long grain-to-long grain glue joint, only a single screw is needed for reinforcement.

Evenly space the two center shelf slats between the outer ones, then countersink and secure them with a pair of 1½" screws in each end. (**PHOTO 7**)

For the tabletop slats, glue and screw a ¾" x 1" cleat to the upper end stretchers. (**PHOTO 8**)

Arrange the four tabletop slats presentation-side down on your worksurface, using spacers to set the gap between them, and clamp together to keep them aligned. (My 2x4s were 3¾" wide, so some ⁵⁄₁₆" pieces of scrap set the gaps just right for a 16" tabletop.)

Upend the cart frame onto the

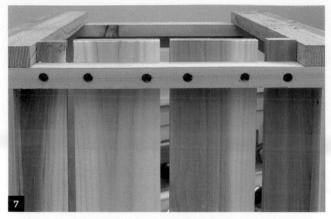

7

Here's how the hole pattern for the completed shelf will look.

8

Attach the cleats for the tabletop slats at the top edge of each upper end stretcher.

9

Drill a pair of evenly spaced, angled holes to secure the outer tabletop slats.

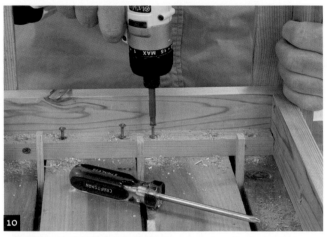

10

Drill countersunk holes through the cleat, then drive in 1½" exterior-grade screws to secure the tabletop.

tabletop and center it, then mark the location. Remove the frame and run a bead of glue along the top of the front/back stretcher, then replace the frame on your marks. Countersink a pair of evenly spaced angled pilot holes through the inner face of the front/back stretcher and drive in 1½" screws to secure those slats. (**PHOTO 9**)

Attach the remaining tabletop slats with a pair of countersunk 1½" screws, as in **PHOTO 10**.

MAKE IT MOBILE

To add wheels to the cart we'll first attach four mounting blocks to the underside, tucked neatly into each of the corners. These blocks are stable 3½" x 3½" squares cut from a pine

2x4, glued and clamped into place until dry. (**PHOTO 11**) My cedar 2-bys were 1¾" thick, so to keep these blocks flush with the stretchers I used regular pine with a thickness of 1½". Be sure to check for, and wipe off, any glue squeeze-out that may go between the gaps of the shelf.

When the blocks have dried, place a wheel on each corner and mark the screw locations, then drill pilot holes and attach the wheels with #12 x 1¼" screws, as in **PHOTO 12**. I've used two regular and two locking wheels, with the locking ones oriented to the front of the cart. Also, I opted for 3" wheels here, which will better handle bumps and cracks on a concrete patio, brick or landscaping pavers and decks. If you'll be using your cart on a per-

fectly smooth surface, you may prefer a smaller wheel.

FINISHING THOUGHTS

I've sanded all corners but left most of the surfaces rough, as I really like the look of rough cedar on outdoor furnishings. However, it's a good idea to smooth the rough tabletop to make it considerably easier to clean and keep clean when cooking, and remove potential splinters from the most-handled areas. I smoothed mine by giving the boards a quick run through a planer, followed by sanding with #100-grit paper. Because I'll be handling the cart mostly by the tabletop edges, I also sanded those to remove splinters.

Cedar weathers wonderfully, ac-

Face-glue the wheel mounts onto the underside of the cart shelf.

Drill pilot holes, then attach all four wheels at the cart corners. Be sure the locking wheels are on the same side.

quiring a silver/gray patina as it ages, and no finish is absolutely required. However, you can keep the bright natural cedar color a bit longer if you give the cart a protective coat of an outdoor deck sealer, such as Thompson's WaterSeal or similar product. A sealer also helps repel stains caused by grease splashes from the grill or dripped food.

As noted earlier, cedar dimensions can vary. The 2x4s I got measured 3¾" wide, and with gaps of ⁵⁄₁₆" between them my tabletop came out at 16" on the nose. However, the 2x4s

you get may be closer to a traditional 2x4 width of 3½". If that's the case, you'll need to make adjustments. You could simply make the tabletop narrower, or you could increase the gap between the tabletop slats to ½" to achieve the 16" width. As an alternative, you could also rip the 2x4s to an even 3" width and use five across instead of the four used here. Five 3" slats spaced ¼" apart would give you a 16"-wide top.

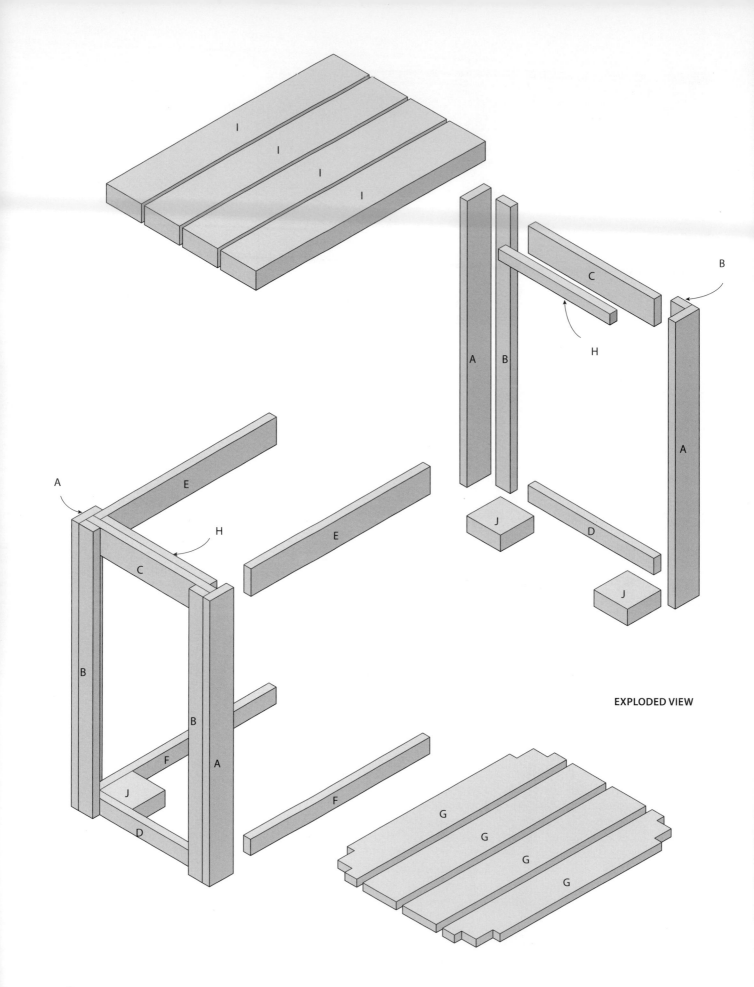

EXPLODED VIEW

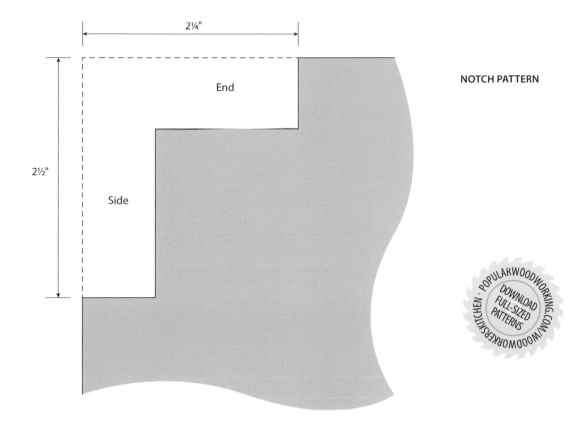

NOTCH PATTERN

2¼"

2½"

End

Side

DOWNLOAD FULL-SIZED PATTERNS

POPULARWOODWORKING.COM/WOODWORKERSKITCHEN

GRILL CART CUT LIST

Overall Dimensions: 16" deep x 24" wide x 31¼" tall

REF	QTY	PART	STOCK	THICKNESS	WIDTH	LENGTH
A	4	Leg, Wide Sides	Cedar	¾"	2½"	26"
B	4	Leg, Narrow Sides	Cedar	¾"	1½"	26"
C	2	Upper End Stretchers	Cedar	¾"	2½"	13¼"
D	2	Lower End Stretchers	Cedar	¾"	1½"	13¼"
E	2	Upper Front/Back Stretcher	Cedar	¾"	2½"	18¾"
F	2	Lower Front/Back Stretcher	Cedar	¾"	1½"	18¾"
G	4	Shelf Slats	Cedar	¾"	3½"	22"
H	2	Tabletop Cleats	Cedar	¾"	1"	11¾"
I	4	Tabletop Slats	Cedar	1¾"	3¾"	24"
J	4	Wheel Mounts	Cedar	1½"	3½"	3½"

NOTES:

Parts A, C and E are standard Western red cedar 1x3. Actual dimensions ¾" x 2½".

Parts B, D and F are standard Western red cedar 1x2. Actual dimensions ¾" x 1½".

Part G is standard Western red cedar 1x4. Actual dimensions ¾" x 3½".

Part I is standard Western red cedar 2x4. Actual dimensions 1¾" x 3¾".

Part J is standard pine 2x4. Actual dimensions 1½" x 3½".

ADDITIONAL HARDWARE:

3" Wheels, Locking (2 needed)

3" Wheels, Non-locking (2 needed)

OPTIONAL HARDWARE:

Utensil Hooks

Bottle Opener

Lazy Susan

WHENEVER ANYONE CALLS ME lazy, I always have a response ready: "I'm not lazy. I'm efficient." And that perfectly describes a lazy Susan.

I suppose you could make an argument that the circular table accessory that today bears some unlucky lady's name (who was this Susan person, anyway?) is a laborsaving device, but it's much more. You can use it as a tray to carry condiments and other items, or even a whole meal, from kitchen to table. By keeping everything accessible to everyone at the table with a light spin, it eliminates needless getting up and down as well as excessive reaching across the table – a real plus with spill-prone youngsters at the table. For items like a turkey or large roast, it facilitates knife use for effective carving. There's nothing lazy about them.

I intend to use this one on our patio, and so made it with western red cedar that matches our picnic table and benches, but any wood – soft or hard – is appropriate. No issues with food contact either, so it doesn't matter if the wood is open- or closed-grain. I did opt to make the base of heavier oak for better balance, but that's optional.

This is a simple project with only two workpieces, a large wooden circle that forms the spinning platter and a smaller circle for the base. Between them is the key to the spinning function, a ball bearing-loaded double ring appropriately called lazy Susan hardware (or mechanism). These are inexpensive and can be found through any woodworking supplier and many home centers. They come in a range of diameters, but a 9" mechanism works well here.

LAMINATE THE WORKPIECES

At 15" in width and with no support at the edges, the platter would be very prone to warping if it was made from a single piece of wood even if you could find a piece that wide, so we'll laminate the platter and base from narrower pieces. Alternating the growth rings in the glue-up will

Trim off any bad edges to prepare for the glue-up.

Apply glue to the board edges, and clamp up the panel till dry.

minimize warping.

Begin by jointing the edges of your stock for a good gluing surface on a jointer or table saw, as in **PHOTO 1**. Western red cedar is very soft and your lumber may have picked up a number of dents, dings and gouges on the outer edges in shipping and or in the racks, so cutting a fresh edge is usually mandatory for glue-ups with cedar. If there are potentially loose knots on the edge, these should be cut off, too, as you can see in the photo. The exact width and number of boards you use to create the platter workpiece isn't important, but allow

a bit extra – maybe an inch or so all around – and cut the platter to size later.

Apply glue to the mating edges and, making sure to alternate the grown rings, clamp up the boards till dry. (**PHOTO 2**) Repeat the process for laminating the base workpiece.

When the assembly has dried, remove it from the clamps and level the surface. In **PHOTO 3**, I'm using a random orbit sander, but you could also use a wide planer or any combination of a hand plane, scraper and sanding. At only 11" wide, I smoothed and leveled the smaller base with a quick

3

Sand both sides of the panel flat and smooth.

4

Draw the platter circle with a large compass or, as here, with a shop-made trammel.

5

Cut out both circles on the band saw, or with a jigsaw, then sand the edges smooth.

6

Starting with the base, mark the hardware mounting holes, plus one of the larger access holes.

trip or two through my planer.

Make a quick 15"-diameter trammel out of any thin piece of wood by drilling a pencil hole in one end and driving a nail 7½" from the hole, then use this to scribe a 15" circle on the workpiece, as in **PHOTO 4**. By the way, sharp eyes will recognize this thin strip as the piece I'm trimming off the board back in **PHOTO 1**, once again proving that there's no such thing as scrap.

Cut out the round platter on a band saw, as in **PHOTO 5**, or with a jigsaw. Repeat the process for the base workpiece.

ASSEMBLY TRICKS

If you've never made a lazy Susan before you may wonder how the hardware is attached. Since all the screws have to be on the inside between the two circular pieces – a space only as high as the hardware is thick – how do you drive the screws into both pieces? The key is that the hardware has a series of access holes stamped directly through the metal along with the screw holes. Here's how that'll work.

Start by centering the hardware on the top (inside) surface of the base. Pencil marks through the screw holes – for a 9" mechanism there

should be four holes – for drilling pilot holes for the screws. (**PHOTO 6**) At this time, also pencil in one of the larger access holes tucked inside the mechanism. It doesn't matter which one. These are a little hard to reach, but you should be able to trace most of the hole which will act as a drilling guide.

Now, drill pilot holes on your marks for four #10 x ½" screws. For the larger access hole, however, drill all the way through the base. A Forstner bit is best for this, and don't forget to back up the cut with some scrap to prevent tear-out.

Place the hardware on the base

7 Drill pilot holes for mounting, as well as the access hole, then line the hardware up and screw into place.

8 With the base centered atop the inverted platter, drive screws through the access hole to complete the assembly.

and line up the four screw pilot holes, which should automatically line up the access hole as well. (**PHOTO 7**) Drive in four screws to attach the hardware to the base.

Invert the base assembly atop the underside of the platter and center it. Rotate the base until you can see the first screw hole on the platter side of the metal mechanism and mark through it onto the wood. Keep turning the base until you've marked all four screw locations. Put the base aside for a moment, drill pilot holes, and then line up the base on the holes you just drilled, sighting once

again through the access hole. Now, just drive the four screws home in turn through the access hole as you rotate the base. You'll note in **PHOTO 8** that I have a magnetic pickup tool handy – unless your drill bit is magnetized there's a good chance you'll drop the screw down into the hole once or twice. The pickup tool makes it easy to retrieve the screw and try again.

That's all there is to it. At this point, all you need is the finish of your choice. There's a good chance food will get on this – you'll use it at the center of the table after all – so

a couple coats of polyurethane is a good option.

I chose the diameter of 15" because it was just the right size for our picnic table. However, alter the size of your lazy Susan anyway you want. The 9" mechanism used here is about average size, but you'll find both larger and smaller hardware. The style and shape of the mechanisms may vary, as well as screw and access hole locations, but the general process of attaching the hardware will remain the same as presented here.

LAZY SUSAN CUT LIST

Overall Dimensions: 1⅞" high x 15" wide

QTY	PART	STOCK	THICKNESS	WIDTH	LENGTH
1	Platter	Cedar	¾"	15"	15" (a)
1	Base	Oak	¾"	11"	11" (a)

NOTES:

(a) Dimensions listed are finished sizes after rounding. Allow a bit extra working room when gluing up the laminated workpieces.

ADDITIONAL MATERIALS:

9" Lazy Susan Hardware (1 needed)

ABOUT THE AUTHOR

Originally a broadcast professional, A.J. Hamler has been a writer and editor for more than two decades, primarily in the areas of woodworking and home improvement. Hamler's articles have appeared in most of the woodworking and home-improvement magazines in the field, while his most recent books include "Build It With Dad" (Popular Woodworking Books, 2015) "Birdhouses and More" (Popular Woodworking Books, 2014) and "Civil War Woodworking Volume II" (Linden Publishing, 2014). He also served as editor of "The Collins Complete Woodworker" (HarperCollins/ Smithsonian, 2007), and wrote the shooting script for the DVD "Plumbing Projects 1-2-3" (Home Depot, 2008). Not all of Hamler's work is nonfiction – writing as "A.J. Austin," he has published two science-fiction novels and numerous short stories. When not in his workshop or fixing something around the house, Hamler enjoys Civil War re-enacting, gourmet cooking, and performing as a stage and voice-over actor.

Distributed in Canada by Fraser Direct
100 Armstrong Avenue
Georgetown, Ontario L7G 5S4
Canada

Distributed in the U.K. and Europe by
F+W Media International, LTD
Pynes Hill Court
Pynes Hill
Rydon Lane
Exeter
EX2 5SP

Tel: +44 1392 797680

Visit our website at popularwoodworking.com or our consumer website at shopwoodworking.com for more woodworking information.

Other fine Popular Woodworking Books are available from your local bookstore or direct from the publisher.

ISBN-13: 978-1-4403-4600-2

20 19 18 17 16   5 4 3 2 1

Editor: *Scott Francis*
Cover Designer: *Daniel T. Pessell*
Interior Designer: *Angela Wilcox*
Production Coordinator: *Debbie Thomas*

a content + ecommerce company

READ THIS IMPORTANT SAFETY NOTICE

To prevent accidents, keep safety in mind while you work. Use the safety guards installed on power equipment. When working on power equipment, keep fingers away from saw blades, wear safety goggles to prevent injuries from flying wood chips and sawdust, wear hearing protection and consider installing a dust vacuum to reduce the amount of airborne sawdust in your woodshop. Don't wear loose clothing or jewelry when working on power equipment. Tie back long hair to prevent it from getting caught in your equipment. People who are sensitive to certain chemicals should check the chemical content of any product before using it. The authors and editors who compiled this book have tried to make the contents as accurate and correct as possible. Plans, illustrations, photographs and text have been carefully checked. All instructions, plans and projects should be carefully read, studied and understood before beginning construction. Due to the variability of local conditions, construction materials, skill levels, etc., w the author nor Popular Woodworking Books assumes any responsibility for any accidents, injuries, damages or other losses incurred resulting from the material presented in this book. Prices listed for supplies and equipment were current at the time of publication and are subject to change.

METRIC CONVERSION CHART

To convert	to	multiply by
Inches	Centimeters	2.54
Centimeters	Inches	0.4
Feet	Centimeters	30.5
Centimeters	Feet	0.03
Yards	Meters	0.9
Meters	Yards	1.1

Ideas ■ Instruction ■ Inspiration

Receive FREE downloadable bonus materials when you sign up
for our FREE newsletter at popularwoodworking.com.

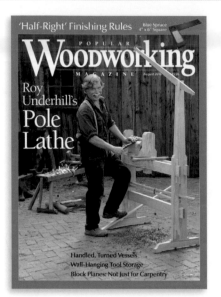

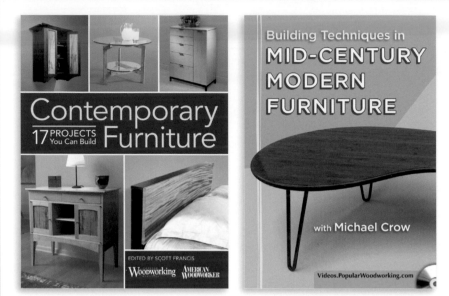

Find the latest issues of *Popular Woodworking Magazine* on newsstands, or visit **popularwoodworking.com**.

These and other great Popular Woodworking products are available at your local bookstore, woodworking store or online supplier. Visit our website at **shopwoodworking.com**.

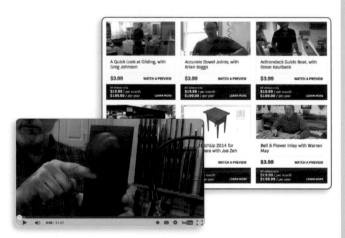

Popular Woodworking Videos

Subscribe and get immediate access to the web's best woodworking subscription site. You'll find more than 400 hours of woodworking video tutorials and full-length video workshops from world-class instructors on workshops, projects, SketchUp, tools, techniques and more!

videos.popularwoodworking.com

Visit our Website

Find helpful and inspiring articles, videos, blogs, projects and plans at **popularwoodworking.com**.

 For behind the scenes information, become a fan at **Facebook.com/popularwoodworking**.

 For more tips, clips and articles, follow us at **twitter.com/pweditors**.

 For visual inspiration, follow us at **pinterest.com/popwoodworking**.

 For free videos visit **youtube.com/popwoodworking**.